"This naked, poignant, and masterfully written memoir of a spiritual awakening will rank among the classics of the genre. Anyone who is lucky enough to read this magnificent testimony will find in it a companion, a teacher, and a guide to the greatest mystery of all: the unfolding of the golden self within the struggles and complexities of the human journey. *Unmasking the Rose* is one of the most amazing and powerful books I have ever read."
— Eryk Hanut, author of *The Road to Guadalupe: A Modern Pilgrimage to the Goddess of the Americas*

"*Unmasking the Rose* is a poetic, loving, remarkable, and beautifully written account of one woman's encounter with the great spiritual energies that underlie the universe and ourselves. In showing how these powerful, intelligent spiritual energies can transform us in the very midst of our everyday lives, Dorothy Walters has done a great service to all spiritual seekers, especially to those who encounter the great and sometimes disturbing power of these mysterious inner energies."
— Jim Marion, author of *Putting on the Mind of Christ*

"Dorothy Walters explores the inner tuning and harmony of energy as it unfolds the mysteries of life. This reflective journal awakes our imagination and spiritual awareness."
— Don Campbell, author of *Music and Miracles* and *The Roar of Silence*

"After reading Dorothy Walters's book, I pondered on the thought that perhaps she is a modern-day Bodhisattva. Walters's words weave a design of heartfelt personal experience that reflect a personal knowing of the God within."
— Rev. Toni G. Boehm, Ph.D., author of *Embracing the Feminine Nature of the Divine: Integrative Spirituality Heralds the Next Phase of Conscious Evolution* and *One Day My Mouth Just Opened: Reverie, Reflection, and Rapturous Musings on the Cycles of a Woman's Life*

"Many people believe, mistakenly, that spiritual awakening is all a matter of 'love, light, and bliss.' But as Dorothy Walters's experience reveals, and as many spiritual disciplines maintain, it can be a process that is perplexing and painful. *Unmasking the Rose* is a valuable chronicle of the complexities of spiritual growth. It will help many people make sense of the challenges they encounter in their own spiritual growth."
— Larry Dossey, M.D., author of *Healing Beyond the Body* and *Healing Words*

"Dorothy Walters's *Unmasking the Rose* provides an exquisitely rich and intimate view of her journey through life, culminating in the profoundly transformative processes engendered by kundalini awakening. The tremendous wisdom she has garnered she shares with humility and grace. There is such a wealth of insight, practical lessons, and expressions of sublime love and ecstasy that readers will want to savor this work slowly and repeatedly. She has the wisdom not to approach this ultimate divine power through the domineering patriarchically skewed techniques found in the popular forms of Kundalini yoga. Instead, she takes the mystic's path, the path of the Lover guided by the Beloved, and is rewarded beyond measure by the Goddess Kundalini."

—Lawrence Edwards, Ph.D.

"Dorothy has braved the Holy Fires for decades of her life without ever losing her way, accepting even the harshest, most searing ordeals as a doorway on the heart of her Beloved. Read even a few pages of this blessed book and you will understand better why great women mystics like Mirabai and Elizabeth of the Trinity endured every kind of mystical experience imaginable, for Dorothy brings the language of our times to precisely the same plane of radically intense experience.

Post-Jungian, savvy, and crystal clear, her descriptions show why and how women fall in love with God and discover the sacred inner Truth that lover, beloved, and Divine Beloved are one. *Unmasking the Rose* should be a requirement in all courses on women's mystics. It will be the first book my students read next summer for a course on the Divine Feminine."

—Mary Ford-Grabowsky, author of *Prayers for All People* and
  Sacred Voices: Essential Women's Wisdom Through the Ages

"Inspirational, casually lyrical, *Unmasking the Rose* is an uncommon memoir that promises a voyage of marvelous discovery for any willing reader.

"To rise above personal subjective entanglements and despair, and to cope with traumas of war, cancer, and plague, Dorothy Walters urges us to move into a new era of elevated consciousness so that a divine tenderness can pour into us, aiding us to heal ourselves, each other, and ultimately the world in a vibrant outpouring of all encompassing love."

—Leila Hadley, author of *Give Me The World*
  and *Journey with Elsa Cloud*

"If the realms of exploration in the new millenium are to be the cosmos without and within us, then this fascinating and meticulous account makes Walters a most courageous forerunner in exploring our inner universe. This book is virtually a revelation of what lies ahead for human consciousness!"

—Alice O. Howell, author of *The Dove in the Stone*
  and *The Web in the Sea*

UNMASKING THE
ROSE

A RECORD OF A KUNDALINI INITIATION

DOROTHY WALTERS

HAMPTON ROADS
PUBLISHING COMPANY, INC.

Cover design by Steve Amarillo
Cover art © Tony Baker/Brand X Pictures/Picture Quest

Hampton Roads Publishing Company, Inc.
1125 Stoney Ridge Road
Charlottesville, VA 22902

434-296-2772
fax: 434-296-5096
e-mail: hrpc@hrpub.com
www.hrpub.com

If you are unable to order this book from your local
bookseller, you may order directly from the publisher.
Call 1-800-766-8009, toll-free.

Library of Congress Catalog Card Number: 2002100966
ISBN 1-57174-301-4
10 9 8 7 6 5 4 3 2 1
Printed on acid-free paper in Canada

Grateful acknowledgement is made for permission to quote from
the following:

Andrew Harvey, *Love's Fire: Recreations of Rumi,* 1988.

Andrew Harvey, Conari Press, Andrew Harvey and Anne Baring,
"Preparing to Meet the Goddess," by Dorothy Walters, *The
Divine Feminine: Exploring the Feminine Face of God
Around the World,* 1996.

Dover Publications, Inc., *The Serpent Power,* Arthur Avalon (Sir
John Woodroffe), 1974.

Hohm Press, "A Golden Haze or Halo," "Rainbows," and "A
Hollow Throat" by Dorothy Walters, from *Marrow of Flame:
Poems of the Spiritual Journey,* 2000.

To the Inner Guru
and
to all who may encounter the goddess
Kundalini
in all her abiding majesty and might

Contents

Acknowledgements

Andrew Harvey, for his unfailing encouragement, protection, guidance, and love. His presence became the "moment which changed everything."

Eryk Hanut, who stood like a beacon of support throughout.

Jeannine Keenan, fellow adventurer on the kundalini path, who found in this book a mirror of her own experience, and shared her delight and wise suggestions.

Patricia Lay-Dorsey, who gave generously of her time, knowledge, and talent to help make this a better tale.

Kit Kennedy, my longtime friend and writing buddy, who kept urging me to move forward.

Jan Elvee, who read it and shared her valuable suggestions and insights.

Karen Kidwell, who helped me get through the experience by sharing her own thoughts and wisdom.

Gina Barnett, for her unfailing enthusiasm and support.

Stephanie Marohn, who gave me a welcome boost over the wall.

Carol Konek, who read this book and liked it, even when it was yet unformed and struggling to be born.

Lawrence Edwards, who shared generously of his wisdom and experience.

Richard Leviton, my editor, who showed me the way.

Foreword

by Andrew Harvey

Near the end of *Unmasking the Rose,* her extraordinarily clear, poignant, and magisterially written memoir of her kundalini awakening, Dorothy Walters writes, "Our world today is at once a theater of disaster and a stage for universal transfiguration. We are at once Christ hanging on the cross and the splendor of the reawakened self." A few lines later, trying to sum up her whole journey, Dorothy writes, "I realized that mine was not merely a private experience but part of a larger process of planetary awakening, of bringing the body and spirit into alignment with divine love unlike anything humanity had previously known. This, I sensed, was the moment in history we had awaited so long. I felt deeply privileged to be a participant in this difficult but immensely significant process of human transfiguration."

In her characteristically humble but direct way, Dorothy Walters is pointing both to the inner meaning of the Apocalypse we are living through and to the possible outcome of its agonies. Our world crisis is at once a horrible and protracted death of all ancient institutions and ways of thinking and a potential birth, on a massive and unprecedented scale, of a new humanity, divinely conscious and divinely inspired, whose creativity and sacred passion could transfigure everything we now understand about human life.

Dorothy Walters knows that this "birth" is by no means certain: the forces of Darkness and Ignorance ranged against it are immense and immensely powerful and will not be beaten back or transformed except by an unprecedented effort of will, love, and surrender to Divine Wisdom and Force in all arenas and all dimensions.

Dorothy Walters also knows that amidst all the chaos and horror of our time, humanity is being given a unique and possibly final opportunity to wake up, not only to its ethical and moral responsibilities toward all life, but to the possibility of living a wholly different, divinised life on Earth, cocreating with the Divine and for the Divine a new world. The Divine, Walters knows, is flooding our world with grace, revelation, and power to awaken and transfigure humanity and help it transcend the destructive dualism both of materialism and of a religiosity addicted to transcendence and an otherworldly vision of God that degrades the body, sexuality, and the creation. In the middle of a crisis that seems to threaten everything, the Divine is holding out to humanity a challenge—the challenge, here on Earth and in a body, to embrace astounding possibilities of incarnating the divine energies and working with them to transform the earth into the living mirror of the Love and Justice of the One.

Dorothy Walters knows these things not from book learning or from mystical piety but because she has experienced them. She has experienced them in the core of her life and in the cells of her body. She has experienced both the apocalyptic terrors of our time and the glorious ferocities of what she calls Divine Love's "relentless alchemy." In her fifties her entire life changed when she had a sudden, completely unforeseen, and transforming kundalini awakening. As *Unmasking the Rose* shows, this initiated a long period of struggle and sometimes bewildering and excruciating integration and adaptation. For, as Dorothy writes, "This, like all human experiences, is mixed. We falter, we lose 'control' (which is by way of not controlling). Our energies go awry, we feel pain where before we sensed ecstasy . . . we walk always on a tightly drawn rope, swaying now this way, now that, occasionally catching our balance and holding it for an interval as our body moves across the immeasurable chasm below." Despite all the complexities and obstacles she encountered, however, Dorothy never lost hope or the passion to explore in ever deeper and ever more precise ways the Mystery that had claimed and possessed her. Now, in her early seventies, she radiates a gentle serenity and strength that give her witness to the workings of Love's "relentless alchemy," the unshakable authority of lived, and lived-through truth.

This witness is Dorothy Walters' extremely precious gift to all of us. She shows us not only *what* she knows but all the different stages and nuances of *how* she came to know it. Such a gift is priceless, for what we all now need is not more "mystical writing," or more "inspired utterances" (the bookshelves of our libraries are already groaning with both the radiant and fake versions of these) but no-nonsense, tough-minded, and generous-hearted *accounts* of *how* the process of transfiguration actually works—as far as that can be described in words—how it demands and tests and how, slowly and mysteriously, it comes to change everything, and go on and on changing everything.

This is what *Unmasking the Rose* so wisely, carefully, and reverently gives us, in a form ideally variegated so as to negotiate and reveal all the different levels of experience and in a prose (and occasionally verse) of exemplary clarity and lack of pretension. Dorothy's journey was a lonely one; for many years there was no one she could turn to for understanding or advice. It is just this extreme solitude, however—and the wild inner courage that it required to pursue so profound an awakening—that give Dorothy's meditations and descriptions their sense of vivid discovery and their bright, fierce, fresh truth. What Dorothy has learnt, she has had to learn for herself and test repeatedly in and on herself; books, and later, certain friends and spiritual mentors helped, but essentially, like most mystical pioneers, Dorothy has been the chemist under God of her own transformation in the laboratory of her life. What must have been intensely difficult for her was, however, the condition for finding and testing those truths she is able to share with us, clear diamonds brought up from a depth of fire-streaked darkness shaped by prolonged, sometimes even intolerable, pressure.

Hold these diamonds now in the palm of your heart and turn them so their light can pierce and irradiate you. Let their dazzle remind you of the infinite wealth of your true nature and your infinite capacity for growth in and under God. Let them inspire you to join the hundreds of thousands of others who now know both the depth of the desperation of our time and the truth of the Birth that it is struggling against vast odds to prepare. Let them give you too the courage to risk the Great Adventure of bringing your soul and body "into alignment with Divine Love." As Dorothy Walters so beautifully and accurately writes, "Constantly, we must turn up our limited receivers to admit higher and higher frequencies, to allow entry to ever more intense vibration streams from the infinite source. . . . Everything is a dance of light and within that dance we find our world of appearances— our visual imagery, our sounds, our inner sensations. And underlying all this is the source, which will speak to us and move us if we pause to attend."

—June 26, 2001, Nevada

What if you slept? And what if, in your sleep, you dreamed? And what if, in your dream, you went to heaven and there plucked a strange and beautiful flower? And what if, when you awoke, you had the flower in your hand? Ah, what then?

Samuel Taylor Coleridge, *Notebooks*

Introduction

How We Are Apprehended and Claimed by the Invisible

When I was in my early fifties, something happened to me that changed my life forever. I did not go out of my body and float beneath the ceiling, I did not fly down a tunnel toward a lighted figure waiting at the end. This experience was something other, something almost no one in my circle had heard of at the time, and which I knew only by rumor, brief allusions in certain texts, and one autobiographical account by an Indian mystic.

The name of what occurred is kundalini awakening. *Kundalini* is a Sanskrit word meaning "coiled." According to ancient seers, the kundalini energy resembles a snake resting (for most of us) at the base of the spine. When it is roused, it raises its head and climbs upward, activating various energy centers (chakras, or "wheels") as it goes. The student is cautioned to approach this process warily, for premature awakening can easily lead to imbalance of the system. Acute illness, even death, as well as major psychological disturbance, can result. The practitioner is warned to proceed cautiously under the supervision of an experienced teacher, one pure of heart and well versed in the nuances of energetic transformation. The reward of successful arousal is ineffable bliss and union with the divine—in other words, enlightenment itself.

Now, my kundalini experience did not follow such a pattern. I was, at the time, fifty-three years old. I was living in Kansas teaching English and women's studies in a state university more dedicated to the production of engineers and M.B.A.s than in supporting the humanities. I had never meditated or done yoga. I lived primarily in my head, not in my body. I had never even had a massage.

I had in this life, just as I have always done wherever I have been, constructed a secret universe, an inner world to serve as a refuge from the hostile elements outside. My first secret world, that of childhood, was simply the world of books and nature. In the woods near my house I sensed an unknown but compelling presence, a reality unlike any I encountered elsewhere. At home I read, and then spent long hours dreaming by the fire of my imaginary encounters. Then in my teens, I was introduced to a Church whose beliefs and practices went so far beyond the familiar institutions of my time that I felt I had been inducted into a secret society. My next experience of the hidden arose from living as a young adult as a lesbian. For me, this was a totally private experience, which had nothing to do with public revelation or political involvement. Indeed, in those days, even friends who recognized each other as lesbian sisters often did not acknowledge the discovery to one another.

Then, when I was in my forties, I began to explore still other unfamiliar realms. Once more, I was seduced by books, but now the authors were writers such as Carlos Castaneda, Jane Roberts, Carl Jung, Joseph Campbell, Mircia Eliade, and John Blofeld. I plunged into a deep study of W. B. Yeats, where I discovered the Golden Dawn and the lure of communicating with invisible spirits. (The Golden Dawn was an occult society in which Yeats participated.) By now my partner Kate and I were in a state of psychic merge; we could make the letters on the Ouija board flash with iridescent light, as the planchette flew around spelling out tantalizing answers to our questions. But one night a very startling message came through, one that frightened and disturbed us both. We renounced our project, and I returned to my teaching pursuits.

So when, after several years of avoiding psychic and/or intense spiritual encounters, I was (it seemed) singled out and captured by a new spiritual energy, one that appeared to originate within my body, though connected in some mysterious way to an outside force, I felt that something novel had entered my life. It took many years before I realized that what was now happening was linked to—indeed, it was a direct consequence of—all the prior events of my life, as if an inner intention, thwarted at one gateway, had simply withdrawn, and later, at the propitious time, entered swiftly through a different door, seizing me and claiming me as its own.

For once kundalini flashes upward through the channels, once it floods the higher centers, unlocking the crown center to receive the streaming effulgence of the light beyond, one knows, forever and indisputably, that the minute atom that carries our name is but a fiction, a tale repeated by the (small) self to the Self to lure us into the belief of separate identity, until the dream-armor is shattered and nothing remains but silence and being.

I knew almost nothing of this strange power called kundalini other than that it is the essential energies of the being, which lie collected at the base of the spine, coiled like a serpent. Kundalini is traditionally imaged not only as a snake, but also as a goddess who awakens. (Indeed, She is held by some to be the *Mahadevi* ("goddess of goddesses"), the life force of the universe itself.) According to the ancient texts, She may be experienced in her fullness only when She rises to the very top of the head and there unites with Shiva, the cosmic awareness that sustains the universe and all its elements. When this union occurs, the crown will "open" and fill with the delight of "a thousand petals unfolding." Thus, the tradition holds, after many years of dedicated practice, the initiate may attain enlightenment, blissful union with the divine.

My awakening, on the other hand, was abrupt and unforeseen, my life transformed in a single instant of grace. From one point of view, I was totally unprepared to be plunged into such an unfamiliar state. From another, I had been preparing my entire life for this transition, and the actual event was merely the culmination of circumstances that had built as if from a foreordained plan. In any event, I was plunged into a time of unimaginable bliss and bodily ecstasy, as well as periods of intense pain and suffering.

Indeed, for the "unprepared" initiate, kundalini exacts a long period of balancing and integration, until the system at last finds it own inner stability and calm. For me, the process was well worth the extremes of its rocky course, for it opened a path of union with the divine. Each deep encounter provided verification of sacred reality, the essence that engenders, enlivens, and sustains all that is, and whose energies can be felt in one's own body, if we but open to them. The "Beloved Within" is not a metaphor. It is a reality to be known and acknowledged in the undeniable evidence of our subjective experience. The "God" who is frequently referred to in this text is not the repressive deity of patriarchal institutions but the Divine Essence, the Beloved as Goddess, or whatever sacred image is closest to one's heart.

This account is drawn from journal entries, kept in notebook form over a period of years, so it includes a variety of voices and tones—narrative, lyric, reflective, and playful. "What I was thinking" was often the primary content of "what I was experiencing," especially in the preliminary stages, the time of preparation. These insights seemed to come as divine teachings, inner instruction as to certain fundamental realities, particular truths the student must grasp as part of the initiation process. And at times, the voice is quite clearly that of the inner teacher, answering specific questions or dictating certain passages.

I have included a few of these early sections of abstract speculation to show how mental exploration can serve as preparation for spiritual renewal, and to reveal the abruptness of the shift from a primarily mental to an essentially experiential focus. Other such entries appear later in the afterword, to emphasize that thought itself—the seeing into the invisible—was a key element in

the experience, in both early and later stages. I have incorporated a few examples of Kate's "Dream Speaking" to show the closeness of the personal relationship, and because they illumine in a special way how the unconscious functions as a vehicle for puns, wordplay, and humor.

In part, the entire experience of kundalini awakening is one of bringing unconscious materials into consciousness. For me, that unconscious is essentially the transpersonal level, present but unknown much of the time. In Jungian terms, this realm of the unknown is the repository of the archetypes, the domain of the collective unconscious, and these, I believe, are not fantasies but realities that can enter our lives to operate in highly significant ways.

I feel that this experience is distinctive in that the kundalini initiate is not, at the end, swallowed by or absorbed into an established spiritual ideology, or wafted out of the world. Her teacher is the inner guide, the solitary voice within who leads to ever higher levels of spiritual discovery. The student (which is me) frequently functions as both subject and interpreter, seeking out hidden implications of such deep-rooted spiritual experience for contemporary society with its many abiding tensions. Though she follows ancient paths, she remains established in the present, able to witness and respond to the events of her time. She acknowledges the shadow on both personal and global levels, and continues to seek the ultimate amid the contingencies of daily experience. Reality is not defined as a closed system. Rather it—the future, and our tenuous vision of truth—remains always open to continuing investigation and dialogue.

Thus nothing in this account, particularly in those sections that involve the processing of ideas, many of which are drawn from the storehouse of perennial wisdom, is intended as a final statement or definitive pronouncement. This book is a record of transactions, not a presentation of "Truth." Some of these transactions are mental (conceptual), some describe personal experience, and some are "dictations" from an unknown source, the "inner guru" ready to answer the deep queries of the self.

Is kundalini awakening, as some suggest, the next stage in the ongoing evolution of human consciousness? Gopi Krishna and others have drawn such radical conclusions, and after careful thought and years of experience, I agree; indeed, universal transformation through stimulation of kundalini appears to be a process well under way. Twenty years ago, it was virtually unheard of outside of the East. Today, it is becoming more and more common across the globe. Various websites offer discussions and personal accounts of myriad seekers who are undergoing inner transformation engendered by kundalini encounters of one sort or another. The word is heard ever more frequently in common discussion.

Although few arrive at the ultimate gate of enlightenment (indeed, the very notion is currently under question), increasing numbers are experiencing this wondrous power in diverse ways. Each encounter is unique, geared to the nature and needs of the novice/initiate. For most, it is an event that transforms the self at the deepest level. It carries us to regions of whose existence we had not dreamed, and yields visions we cannot describe. Kundalini is the source, the point of balance, toward which we all continually struggle. It is indeed a potent healing force for the self and for the world. Manifesting as love, compassion, and oneness, it can carry us to the next stage, humanity transformed and transfigured.

Part 1

Preparation: mind Encounters Mind

The Supplicants

At the throne of God, the angels have no form at all,
but come as pure, raw energy . . .

Sophy Burnham

There are many ways
of approaching the throne.

Some move solemnly,
majestically,
a procession of wisemen
contemplating a final reality.

For others, it is a celebration
of the soul in love trance.
They are caught in a
fiery transformation,
a dancing beyond the reach
of silence or the Word.

Others quietly abase themselves,
moving forward slowly, intent,
imprinting the dust
as they go,
with their bodies' thin shadows.

It was summer, and I was caught up in a passion of writing. Each day I left my office at noon (I was coordinator of a small women's studies program in a mid-western state university) and rushed home to add to an already full notebook.

I was not writing poetry or fiction. Rather, I was composing (or, really, "receiving") entries of another kind, essay/reflections on certain fundamental truths, certain universals of human experience. Topics seemed to arise spontaneously, revelations to pour forth—on what? Sometimes my themes were inspired from recent reading, or were elaborations of key metaphors beginning to emerge in the general consciousness. I was processing, deeply, comprehensively, as if my mind were exploring its own limits, as if some unseen teacher were guiding me in my quest. I was pursuing some reality, not as words arranged in a mechanical order, but as an element to be fused with, assimilated into my own tissue and bone. My discoveries were not necessarily original, but I was claiming certain concepts fully, making them mine.

What, I questioned, is the true distinction between wave and particle, beyond the definitions assigned by physics? Is the one (particle, discrete, segregated) masculine, and the other (wave, flowing, continuous) feminine? If so, do these make some statement about the nature of God, Who includes all contraries and thus can seemingly fuse all opposites into one? What is the essence of the Christ myth, and how does it speak to us now as contrasted, say, with the Demeter-Kore story that so long reigned at Ephesus? In both, the soul is the preeminent concern. But in the one, the central deity figure is trapped and then mutilated, his very flesh nailed to wood, in order that the god, through suffering, may redeem a fallen humanity. In the other, there is also loss and redemption, but grief is outweighed by celebration in rites of renewal, and the goddess is reclaimed for life on this Earth. How are our psyches rearranged by the notion that God might be female rather than male? Is Earth itself an ongoing process of emanation and evolution? Are we indeed fragments thrown forth from some unknowable center, which then draws us back by invisible threads of love?

Outside, the pavements sizzled and the tar melted on the sidewalks. It was hot, one of the most torrid summers ever recorded in the state. Inside my air-conditioned house, I labored in isolation, as if receiving truths from an invisible instructor, as if preparing for some approaching event. What I did not realize was that I was, in fact, being readied for a profound spiritual initiation, that kundalini was already beginning to stir within. And that the moment, when it arrived, would require that I put aside all my "learning" and intellectual striving. That only when I surrendered mind, could I find the thing that my mind was seeking.

I had had initiations before. I think of initiation as an inner event that so transfigures the self that one is indeed a new being thereafter, apprehending with new senses, comprehending with new vision. In earlier times, these transformations were achieved through group ceremony or ritual, perhaps tribal or ecclesiastic. Today, cut off as so many of us are from formal religious affiliation, initiation frequently occurs through a more subjective, inward process. Something previously concealed stirs and presses through, and our lives are turned upside down and inside out, reordered into a new psychic configuration.

A Fisher of Souls

My first initiation occurred when I was sixteen. I was taking classes at the local college, though technically I was still a high school senior. My new English teacher was a poet, a transcendentalist, and a member of the Church of Christ, Scientist. She viewed the world as a tangible manifestation of the divine reality at the core. All things conspired to serve the underlying purposes of Ultimate Good. Her views were confirmed in the writings of Emerson, Wordsworth, and Thoreau (as well as scripture, and the words of Mary Baker Eddy, founder of her Church). The Good, the True, the Beautiful—these were absolutes whose presence constantly unfolded all about us. Through her teaching, she strove to awaken her slumbering students, to alert them to the pull of the higher truth.

Unfortunately, most of her pupils—aspiring public school teachers and would-be high school football coaches—were slow to arouse. For them, the weekly writing assignments were exercises wrung from unwilling brains at the last moment, the class a tedious requirement to be fulfilled on their way to more congenial pursuits. But for me, this woman appeared as an avatar, a human embodiment of certain verities I had occasionally glimpsed in a few authors, such as Whitman, and Plato in the *Republic*. But now she stood before me, the concept embodied in the flesh, the ideal captured in the actuality.

She was, I thought, quite handsome. She was in her early forties, a rather short, plumpish woman, but with a face that was marked with its own inner and outer beauty. Her skin carried a rich color across the high cheekbones. (Could she be part Native American, I wondered. She resembled nothing so much as a proud warrior or chief, aristocratic, self-possessed.) Her jet hair was parted in the center, then swept back in two wings from the rounded forehead and caught in a bun at the nape of her neck. (Or did it only seem so? Was it really short hair arranged to give the effect of a bun?) Her dark eyes twinkled, as if she possessed an inner secret, as if she were a magician about to perform some amazing feat. Her full, mellifluous voice lent each syllable of verse, each phrase, its proper weight and resonance. Being with her was, for me, like entering the presence of a prophet or seer, one of the chosen. I was heady with my discovery—of the person, of the perspective. Art, belief, reality—all cohered in a luminous vision of truth. My idol was a fisher of souls, and I was an instant catch.

Soon I was traveling each Sunday with her, her best friend the drama teacher, and several other students (all crammed into her one-seater coupe) to attend services at her church in the larger city nearby. There we chanted together, "There is no life, truth, intelligence, or substance in matter. God is infinite mind and its infinite manifestation, for God is all in all." We listened not to sermons, but to passages read aloud from the Bible and from Eddy's *Key to the Scriptures* by a male-female pair. Perhaps because of the gender of the founder, women were allowed a particularly prominent role in this religion. When we felt ill, we called Mrs. P., a "reader," who healed through right thinking and concentration on selected passages from the Bible and Eddy's *Key.* Any apparent ailment was labeled a "mistake" that could be corrected through purifying consciousness and readjusting one's inner conviction. Since I was young, and in good health, I had little need to test this assumption.

Frequently, our little band met and drove out before dawn into the Oklahoma countryside, where we walked along deserted country roads. Often the landscape was transformed by snow or frost into another, less familiar setting. The air was crisp and pure, as the sky changed from the blue-black of a crow's wing to the reddish hue of some inner light struggling toward birth. What did we talk about on these star-lit treks? The gracious hand of Good? The gentle healing touch of Love? I felt that something big was approaching in my life, that I was heading toward a precipice and that I would have to fling myself over it to discover what was waiting below.

Our last writing assignment of the semester, about our own most important beliefs, opened me to an awareness I had never fully grasped before. For my topic, I chose the inherent distinction between the deceptive world of manifesting form and the absolute realities that reside invisibly within. This exercise served as a breakthrough experience for me as a young seeker of truth, for in the course of articulating my thoughts, I underwent a classic experience of religious conversion.

I saw, clearly and irrevocably, the futility of a life dedicated to material goals. I pondered once more the myth of Plato's cave, and knew that I would never again confuse shadow and reality. My spirit was in fact "reborn," into a sense of the seamless divine perfection that begets and sustains all things. All I saw around me took on a different hue. The world and its inhabitants now began to shine with intense beauty, as if lit by an inner lamp. I was filled with love for all that was.

It was an archetypal drama of youthful initiation, with familiar features—the beloved elder acting as mentor and guide, the unveiling of truth in a stunning revelation, the assurance that everything had meaning if its text were but read correctly. I did not know that this rite had been enacted for many centuries by countless participants. I only knew that a precious moment had arrived, conferring a grace to be received and welcomed.

But when I was eighteen I went away from home to attend the state university, and in these new surroundings my beliefs weakened. One morning, I awoke to find my throat enflamed and raw. The infirmary diagnosed my problem as strep throat, and put me in isolation for observation. I accepted their treatment, for faith alone was not enough to sustain me in this crisis. Afterward, I never returned to my previous level of commitment. Gradually, I absorbed the values of the more "intellectual" world about me, and lost touch with my earlier convictions.

However, one incident occurred during this period that seemed of special significance. I still sometimes engaged in the once common practice of Bible reading to find answers to various personal or scriptural questions, a technique I had learned from my teacher. Often, these passages seemed to be amazingly relevant. Many times I asked about the true value of the Christian Science approach, and almost always got the same answer: some variant of "By their fruits you shall know them." This time, however, I had asked what my true vocation was. The answer came from a passage in Hebrews: "Called to be a high priest, after the order of Melchizedek."

I was pleased to think of becoming a servant of God. But who was Melchizedek? I had no idea. Long after, I found that within the esoteric tradition Melchizedek was a high priest serving John, the acknowledged head of the mystical "inner orders." In fact, some credit Melchizedek (which is in fact a title, not a name) with having originated certain lineages of occult teaching, both ancient and modern. In any event, the connection is with a hidden, rather than a public, role or tradition.

But in the years that followed, I put spiritual concerns to one side. When I entered graduate school, I concentrated on perfecting that air of skepticism and ironic detachment so prized by many students of the time. We had our enthusiasms—but they were for the intricacies of the New Criticism and the fine points of close textual analysis, not for the potential illumination of a spiritual vision. Our moral perspective was based on a sincere concern for the betterment of society, but we did not subscribe to any particular doctrine or creed. The Bible concerned us not as a sacred text, but as the source of various literary allusions. Art, particularly literature, was our passion and our delight. This era was the golden age of the humanities, and we reveled in the spirit of the time.

Ultimately, I finished my Ph.D. (in English) and took my first university teaching job. I wrote a small book on an emerging literary figure, Flannery O'Connor, but published it too late to win tenure in my department. I then accepted a position teaching English at another, less distinguished university, one offering limited intellectual and cultural stimulation, hence a place where there were few interruptions of my daily round of teaching, reading, and grading papers. I did not suspect that in this unlikely locale, I was to experience the key episode of my life.

During these years—graduate school and those following, when I was in my twenties and thirties—I had developed a pattern of falling in love, always with disastrous consequences. Each time, I committed myself unreservedly to my idealized love image, and each time I was, ultimately, abandoned, left to drown, it seemed, in my own pool of grief. I did not understand how those who had professed love so ardently at one stage could so easily vanish, leaving me to deal with my psychic and emotional wounds as best I could. This pattern repeated three or four times over some twenty years. Inevitably, when I thought I had found stability with a soul mate, an enduring partner, she severed the relationship, and I was alone once more.

My term of suffering was never a matter of weeks or months. It generally persisted for years, and during these times I frequently experienced a clinical depression. My situation was complicated because at that time, same-sex orientation was classed as a major psychological aberration, with the result that one had no one to turn to in time of crisis, neither counselor nor friend. Because of my bad luck in love, I decided not to try again.

But I was still comparatively young (forty-two), and so I fell in love once more. This time, it seemed I had found the true companion I had been seeking. Once again, I felt I had stumbled upon perfection, and, yet another time, I abandoned myself to the intensity of the experience. All the emotional and psychic borders between the two of us seemed to dissolve. Each consciousness flowed easily in and out of the other's awareness, as if we were a single mental unit. We shared each other's dreams, and at times could communicate without speaking. The paranormal became customary in our daily exchange. During this period I discovered the power of the Mother Goddess, and this archetype began to activate within me. At times, in our most intimate moments, my beloved seemed to transform into a deity in my arms. We had reached a tantric level in our relationship, exploring an astonishing state of consciousness that came naturally and unbidden. Our union was complete, or so I thought.

Books had begun to appear that spoke to my continuing interest in hidden things. Carlos Castaneda, the Seth books of Jane Roberts, Joseph Campbell's work on myth, Neumann's study of the Great Mother—I read these with avid attention. I explored the work of W. B. Yeats, poet and occultist, and discovered his powerful connection to esoteric realms. Then something unforeseen occurred.

The Coming of M. Kabal

Kate and I had been together for several years. She was twenty years my junior, and this age difference seemed to increase the intensity of our relationship. We lived in a state of social seclusion—it was a time when loving same-sex partners did not advertise their alliances to society at large. We thus became incredibly close, merged in the fullest sense, our focus centering on our public roles as student and teacher, and our private world of shared experience.

We had experimented with a Ouija board, and we soon found that we could communicate with an ostensible high master. At first, he used the code of "MKBL," which mystified me, but which Kate quickly interpreted as "Master of Kabbalah." Later, we referred to him as "M. Kabal." He led us deeper and deeper into ever more obscure regions, instructing us at times to devise an amulet for protection, or to consult Madame Blavatsky for clarification of some unclear point. Each night our board blazed with an eerie blue-golden light, outlining the letters and our hands as well, as we sought communication with this unknown being from an unseen realm.

Other bizarre events started happening. I began to fall into light trance states in which I would watch symbolic figures appear inwardly and then transform into other related images (as, say, a unicorn becoming a fan of feathers). Often, I incorporated these images into my poetry, which seemed to move to a new level. I wrote of the hero's journey or of the Great Mother, both powerful archetypes beginning to rouse in universal consciousness. Indeed, this period was like a subtle stirring of the universal psychic layer, as if some slumbering human talent for connection with the unseen were being gently reclaimed.

I frequently experienced incandescent lights exploding in my head, or saw swirls of color churning in brilliant display. Kate, more attuned to sound, sometimes heard little bells chinging in our living room, as if beings were passing in and out the (closed) apartment door. One spring morning, I opened my fist and let her smell the invisible violets I carried in my hand. Our telepathic abilities continued to expand. One night, as an experiment, we tried sending each other mental images from a new tarot deck, a version neither of us was familiar with. In fact, we knew little of tarot of any kind. I picked up little as receiver, but when we reversed roles, Kate as the receptor was able to describe with astonishing accuracy five cards in succession. Moreover, the fifth card (the Fool) was in fact the first repeated (I had inadvertently drawn it out a second time); she correctly identified it and announced, "We've had this one before."

Other talents were manifesting. I was now able to observe individual faces changing into shifting versions of themselves, as if I were seeing other incarnations of the subject. One evening, as we finished our session at the Ouija board, I sat quietly and watched Kate's features go forward in time until she seemed to have aged some ten or so years. I was beginning to see auras too. When I looked in the mirror, my face was always enveloped in swirling clouds of red, but around others I consistently saw various shades of purple or violet. Once I watched as a singer's bright magenta aura swelled out during her solo, then shrank abruptly when she sat down.

Kate and I also used to "share" dreams. That is, when we compared notes at breakfast, we often discovered that we had had parallel or complementary dreams. (One night we each dreamed we had returned to an archetypal Eden, where serene animals roamed over green landscapes.)

Kate frequently talked in her sleep, seeming to call up a host of characters who spoke "through her" in an internal drama. One of these was a Welshman from some earlier century who spoke of the marshes and asked about the "bairn." Another was a child who called herself "Big Eddy" (after a gangster hero), who described in poignant detail her life with her mother in a miserable tenement room in New Jersey. The dialogue with "Eddy" continued over three nights until it ended with the death of the mother, and Eddy being sent to a foster home. And once, an unknown woman spoke sorrowfully to "Isho": "Isho, you must never go to Louisville again. I rang the bell for you, Isho. And I wept for you. I wept." (Who was Isho and what had happened to him/her? Was he husband/lover? Had he been killed? Who was the speaker?)

Were these "real" entities—disincarnates, perhaps—floating into Kate's psyche as she drifted off to sleep? Or were they fragments of her subconscious, finding voice as the conscious mind relaxed control? Often these "sleep speakings" came through in a child's voice, with many puns, riddles, jokes, and verses of the sort that children love. I felt that I had direct access to Kate's inner awareness, and so was able to verify Freud's theories about the love of that deep level for wordplay, puns, and the like. Sometimes when she spoke aloud, I answered mentally, and she would respond (again aloud) to my unspoken words.

Early one evening, Kate told me that she had seen a "spirit cat" in our hallway. And that night, as Kate drifted off, the spirit cat spoke to me in a highly imperious tone, explaining that he had come to guard us. Another night, soon after we had visited a psychic reader in California, Kate's human spirit guide announced his presence, in a strong, commanding voice (as she slept). Kate was able to remember this visitation. Her guide was a robed Egyptian, arrayed in colors absolutely pure, hues never seen on Earth. The psychic had told us that Kate and I had an extremely strong connection, and that we were to be together, "even in the interims" between incarnations. Our deep psychological merge and our many paranormal experiences seemed to confirm her observation. We had become a single mental unit.

Communication with the spirit world was not always easy. At the conclusion of one especially dramatic session at the Ouija board, M. Kabal announced that we were "O = O." At first, I felt rebuked, as if we were being dismissed as worthless, but this was not the case. "0 = 0" (I discovered) is used in the Golden Dawn (the early esoteric group that had so fascinated Yeats) to designate a beginner, a student in preparation. In other words, we were started on a path, although not accepted into the inner membership. We were both exhilarated and frightened.

Did the Golden Dawn still operate on the inner planes? Was our guide a trustworthy sponsor? Was he indeed a disembodied kabbalist, one who was master of communication between the realms? Was he in fact the spirit of Yeats? He displayed intimate knowledge of Yeats' life and stylistic preferences, even going so far as to use the formal subjunctive mood on occasion. We never asked him his identity directly, but when we inquired if he knew

Leo Africanus (Yeats' own spirit guide), he answered, "Of course."

By this time, books on the Golden Dawn were becoming available, and with their help, we began to prepare for advancement to the next grade. Among other subjects, we studied the Hebrew alphabet, astrological signs, alchemical processes, and the tarot, with its associated kabbalistic paths. Our "teacher" (M. Kabal), was always courteous, and offered intelligent, rather formal answers to our queries. He was obviously associated with magic: "You must craft the dagger and the cup," he admonished us.

But he did not want our relationship to be put to superficial uses, and was clearly affronted when we asked him the whereabouts of a neighbor's lost billfold. The planchette spelled only gibberish while she (the neighbor) was present, but as soon as she left, M. Kabal protested, "I am not a cheap crystal ball." When we inquired about some long-lost medieval manuscript a colleague was interested in, he did not give the location as we asked, but advised, "I will answer questions of the intellect as well as questions of the soul." His most memorable reply came when I asked if it would be possible to follow this method and a path of meditation at the same time; he cautioned, "Difficult. These are two diverse paths whose ends converge in the winding gyres." ("Gyres" is a term used by Yeats to symbolize the unfolding of various impulses, especially oppositions of various kinds.)

That summer, Kate and I went to Colorado for three months, and something disturbing occurred. When we tried our Ouija board, we received a chilling message, unlike any previous communication: "Take knife, cut arms, legs, of young one." Kate had always been a somewhat reluctant participant in our ongoing experiment, and now she balked entirely. As she pointed out, we didn't know exactly what we were doing or what forces we were dealing with. Perhaps the message was from some intruder. (Kabal had always shown great respect, even a formal courtesy in his responses. Had he not come along with us to Colorado?) Or perhaps this was in fact he, our familiar "instructor," showing his true colors at last. In any event, this was the end of the Ouija experience.

But it was not yet the end of my association with M. Kabal. I continued to prepare alone for the initiation into the Golden Dawn. When the time came a few weeks later, I tested myself (by simply writing out the astrological signs, etc., which I had studied). After some inner imagery, and some circle dancing with my invisible instructors, I went in to view my face in the mirror, and had the shock of this or any lifetime.

As usual, my features were surrounded by a reddish glow, the color of "passionate intensity," certainly the state I was in at that time. When I had performed this exercise in the past, my face would sometimes change into other versions of itself, some better, some worse, from the anxiety-ridden neurotic to the wise woman of exquisite poise. But this time, something different happened. My face seemed to dissolve, and then to go far back in time. Am I witnessing my own death? I wondered. But then the image seemed to recede even further, becoming a mask out of antiquity, a stone image of some ancient, pagan being, with carnal features obscenely leering. I was horrified. I had, it seemed, contacted not the angelic, but the demonic realms. I had turned myself into a gross disfigurement of all I had hoped to be.

I was terrified and appalled. I had tried to raise myself to a higher level, and had succeeded, apparently, in entering the realm of the demonic. I knew that initiates are sometimes given a totally unfamiliar symbol for interpretation, but I had never anticipated something as disturbing as this. I prayed for forgiveness, renounced the Ouija board and the path associated with it, shut the occult books, and severed all ties with the invisible world. After a week or so, I felt restored to grace. The mountains once again reflected their singular luminescence. But my adventure with the "spirit guide" was finished.

I did, however, write a poem about my unnerving experience. When I contemplated the strange image in the mirror, a phrase came to mind: "The Mask of Silenus." I did not know who Silenus was, but later discovered that he was the tutor of Dionysus, and hence the god of initiation through ecstasy. And indeed, it was to be ecstasy of a different kind that would provide my subsequent initiation into the mysteries of kundalini.

I wrote this poem about the encounter:

The Angel

He does not always come
as a white passion
glowing in a dark surround.

Sometimes the face has eyes
burnt through to nothing
with seeing all too long.
The mouth a slit in silence.
The nose an Attic jest.

Who looks here finds no center,
no reassuring sign,
fish token of love:
Behold the mask of Silenus,
gross mirror-mocker
of the Dionysian school,
your father and your guide.

Almost fifteen years later, after the death of my father, I came upon a fuller description of Silenus and his role in early initiation rituals of initiation. In ancient Greece and Rome, young boys, as part of their introduction to manhood, seemed to see their own faces changed to masks of Father Silenus, embodiment of the procreative principle. This was done by a clever mirror trick; often the young initiate was terrified at what he saw in front of him. Somehow, the archetype had also triggered for me, and I, too, was unnerved by what I beheld.

Now, some years later, I was readying myself for yet another major transfiguration, this different from anything I had experienced before. It was as if the gods, denied entry by one portal, will discover another mode of access into the consciousness. I was now fifty-three years old, still teaching in the same university, still with Kate. But the unthinkable was about to occur.

In my journal, I was often writing about ideas, but I also included certain personal experiences, especially those pertaining to unusual states of consciousness. Here are some observations from that period:

Amyl Nitrate

I have been to a party and there—for the first and only time in my life—have sampled amyl nitrate. ("Go ahead," they urged. "This is very mild. It absolutely can't hurt you.") So I, stranger to drugs of any kind, one who "gets high" on a few cups of coffee or two glasses of beer, agreed to "try it," not realizing that it would, rather, "try me." Whether we smoked or inhaled or drank it—I scarcely recall now. Something was passed around. Surely we pressed a vial to our nostrils and inhaled, as if our noses were stopped up, as if we were asthmatic.

Then I relaxed deeply, and listened to music while I watched little dots of light dance in carefully composed geometric patterns in the air. I noted I had two—or more—centers of gravity, and how strange that seemed. I went home and had an inner vision:

The dancers are moving through a spiral labyrinth; we go in, we go out, in the cycle of birth and death, and rebirth. But some go in and do not return. (Do they fall into a black hole at the center?)

Shakti stands before us, waving her six arms in the dance. Her many limbs reveal her nature as a multiple being, for the Mother has many wombs.

Someone (a young male) hurtles across the plane of vision, a powerful karate master or pupil; his energy is intense, potentially destructive.

Flowers are opening, symbols of life, which is ever rooted in sex and nature.

Seeds spew forth in abundance from the flowers: procreation from nature.

How can we fuse with the god of this world in transcendent union?

And so the themes were set for the experience that was to follow.

On Seeing Faces

Although I have seen auras only occasionally, I have frequently seen "faces." That is, I have stared at a countenance until it changed to something other, often appearing as someone from another place or time. (Of course, anyone can do this trick: stare softly but intently at a face—or any given object—and the contours will soften, the outlines give way, and something new will appear in the place of the original.) It may be just a trick of the eyes, or a subtle projection of an inner mental image on an external subject. Or perhaps the new face is something else, a visage from a past life, or a symbolic archetypal image with some special, deep association with the object of contemplation.

The first time I had this experience was with a friend sometime in the 1960s. John and I had been drinking wine and listening to music throughout the evening. He was discoursing on some topic of interest; he was an enthusiastic talker. As I gazed at him, his face began to "melt" into that of a young man of American Revolution times—a pigtailed fellow, with shirt open at the throat, a bit untidy, but someone passionately committed to the revolutionary cause. From time to time, John's own face would "come back," and then a new surge of discourse would bring in the young man. Sometimes (at least once or twice), he changed briefly to a priest in robes.

Two things about John are pertinent here. He is extremely interested in politics (particularly democratic processes) and his religion (Catholic) is of central importance in his life. Were the "images" mere projections of my sense of his character and commitments? Were they, rather, reflections or re-creations of certain former selves, whose interests continue to manifest in the present personality? This seems to be a "chicken-egg" question, and I have the same problem with all accounts of "past lives" that are supposed to explain present personalities. I do not discount the notion of reincarnation entirely, but the ground is tricky here.

During the time when Kate and I were deeply immersed in Ouija work, and I was studying elementary Kabbalah, Tarot, Mother Goddess imagery, and other things, we both experienced numerous psychic phenomena. I saw her at various times in different guises. Once she appeared as a tall, large-boned Spanish male of the nineteenth century: Basque, I thought. This fellow was looking very sad; I felt he was discouraged by the difficulties of political reform. Another time she appeared as a small Swiss male about forty—quiet, sensitive, one who did precise technical work of some sort; he, too, was a political revolutionary.

Often the object of my gaze is a lecturer or performer of some sort. I once saw a young bearded poet turn into a skirted Persian or Assyrian priest/poet of ancient times: he was reciting for his king in a performance at court, in an extremely solemn manner. As I contemplated his shifting features, I discerned the masks of tragedy and comedy flitting over his face, his profile, and the side of his head, as if these images were his attendant spirits.

When Kate Millett, early feminist and cultural historian, spoke at our university, she transformed into a judge, wigged and robed, from another century, as if her passion for justice and righting social wrongs took its inception from another, earlier self.

I was in the audience when novelist/poet Margaret Atwood read at the Modern Language Association Meeting in San Francisco (about 1975), and saw her in many variations. One was a short, stocky, blond Frenchman—he seemed to be a man of little formal education, but one endowed with much native intelligence and wit, who had won his way in the world by virtue of innate talent and sheer drive. I think he was a journalist from the eighteenth or early nineteenth century. He was lacking in polish, but people respected his natural gift for language and his ability to interpret the social scene. He was quite talented in his "country boy" way. Then I saw Atwood's face transform into that of a woman of about fifty, the madam of a bordello, I believe; several other visages flashed by so quickly I could not identify them. She seemed to be a composite of many, many strands.

Once the poet W. S. Merwin turned into a Native American of the far Northeast, or possibly Canada. He possessed rough, primitive features, and wore the headdress of a shaman with buffalo hide and horns. At first I had difficulty making out his identity. At last I thought, "Why, he's an Indian." About five minutes later, Merwin said to the audience, "When I was a child, I always wanted to be an Indian, not a cowboy."

I have also seen my own face change in various ways. From staring intently at my image in the mirror, I have seen a vast range of combinations and permutations, all, however, recognizable as myself. These diverse images reflected the potentials of the being, from fulfillment to failure.

Once, about 1979, I caught a glimpse of a "former me" in a window. I was an Eastern monk, a jolly, uncombed fellow who obviously enjoyed life in his spiritual retreat. Another time, I observed the reflection (again in a window) of a different monk; this man was charming and extremely balanced in mind and body. He smiled warmly. I recognized him as the abbot of a monastery (Eastern), and realized with a bit of a shock that this man was no ascetic. Both of these religious figures had my features, though somewhat modified.

But the most disturbing reflection of self appeared as the "Mask of Silenus," which had so shocked and terrified me.

Disturbing Images

Recently, as I drift off to sleep, various bizarre images arise in consciousness. Animals or animal-like forms with long sinewy necks writhe obscenely. What are these images? Why do they come?

A. (from the inner voice): Like images of death or destruction, these must be encountered in order to be overcome. Once past, they are no longer seen in terms of terror or disgust, but as harmless symbols, void of potency.

Years later, when I read Daughter of Fire, *Irina Tweedie's account of her spiritual awakening, I found that she described a similar period when obscene images besieged her consciousness. I think that this stage has to do with the preliminary arousal of the kundalini energies, before they are fully established in the system. The gods denied are transformed into demons.*

On Love

The truth is, I find myself living at the center of a myth that has outgrown its time. Love, honor, dedication—what have these to do with a world where honor is an upended garbage container and justice a freaky joke? A world where the media channels are jammed with the most random and spurious outpourings, ranging from the loathsome to the trivial. Where the most brilliant literary minds depict a world glimmering in the "phosphorescence of decay," and the artists amuse themselves with infantile obscenities.

This, we are told, is the world of our century, the environs of our time. Yet, must we not struggle privately, by whatever means we can summon, to keep the horror at bay, to maintain, at whatever cost, a private sanctuary where *virtu* in the classical sense is preserved as reality and not derided as travesty.

To proclaim nothing is no guarantee that nothing exists. Any assertion of meaninglessness must be couched in the language of meaning.

So we retreat into the dubious shelter of private love—amid the catcalls, deprecations, and sneers of our contemporaries who insist that it (love) does not, cannot by definition exist, being an illusion bred of adolescent naiveté. Or that it did once exist, but world conditions now exclude it from the list of possibilities. Or that it can exist, but only for a brief and limited period, its own demise well embedded in its life impulse (Blake's "catch joy as it flies," etc.).

As a result of the demythologizing of love, many rush en masse to random couplings with arbitrary partners, to tedious unions with inadequate bedmates, to solitary pleasure or freakish shared solace. All in a headlong press to avoid, or escape, to show themselves at last emancipated from, the horrible shape-changing universally deceptive mask of the thing calling itself love. Thus they trade a countenance for a genital.

Together, we two listened, years ago, as Nancy (in psychic trance) spoke to us of that time we were linked together, in the lost world of the forgotten East, and we, our hearts overflowing, sat quietly, our auras intermingling in a delicate dance overhead.

A Drama I Wrote Myself

Sometimes I wonder in panic, what if my life is a drama I wrote myself? I mean not in the sense of immediate, lived choices, but as a pre-invented, pre-intended narration, a story conceived and then cast with myself as principal, playing from a hidden script.

What have I chosen? Personal loss and suffering from love objects that could not but reject (myself first rejecting myself).

And now we—she and I together—live on the outside, the borders, the land of exile from which we contemplate life but do not share in its communal action. Rather we live a secret existence in a private world whose nature and realities are invisible to the majority (because "they" cannot detect it). We are like worlds within worlds, an unseen "colony of two" within the larger visible unit.

Thus we are at the same time on the "outside" (the excluded) and the "inside" (ourselves being an invisible center, an unperceived universe in the midst of the common world).

The Kabbalists say that before the soul is born, it passes before the throne of God, where it pleads not to be enfleshed. Always, its request is denied.

Once, long ago, I tried to recall the time before my birth. A sense of tranquillity, happiness, and self-content, as if I tended a garden, floated into consciousness. Then came a sense of inevitability, a sentence from which there was no appeal. I knew that I must go into the world to "learn to *be dependent on others.*" To accept the degradation of the dispossessed, to allow the self to merge with and be nourished by the totally not-self. An experience of *humility*. A breaking out of *oneness* as sufficiency into the vulnerability of need.

I came through but had from birth a great sense of loss, grief, and regret. My mother did not want me (though she loved me enough after birth). Together we were trapped in a fated moment, which neither of us wished or controlled.

Only years later did I discover that my mother had intended to abort me, as she had other pregnancies, but that for some reason she had changed her mind at the last minute.

On Coincidence

Certain "coincidences" of our life may be artificial, arising, mainly, from our own manufacture. Other resemblances permit of more objective verification. As, for example, recurrent names or initials of lovers or others who play significant roles in our lives.

It is as if we—or it, or they—or whoever sketched out the preliminary design for our lives—chose certain ornamental motifs, particular designs, cues, symbols, whatever, either to project us to recognition by repetition of the iconic mode, or else that we unconsciously attract to ourselves and are subsequently energized by interaction with certain ideograms, which thus become the heraldry of the self.

What if, in fact, we are merely "receptors" capable of receiving (reproducing) certain patterns of relationship, as occurs, say, in a captured moment of a kaleidoscope, or as energy pulsating in various frequencies? Or, possibly, as in the pattern of a snowflake?

What is the relation of mantras to this notion? Does sound (number) actually translate into design (form)? Does something like this occur within us from "cosmic sources"? Are there cosmic pulsations awakening a sympathetic resonance within?

On Huxley and Drugs

In *The Doors of Perception* (1954), Aldous Huxley describes the mescaline experience, in which "things"—flowers, furniture, clothes—are transformed into ultimate aesthetic phenomena. He was amazed and fascinated, but somewhat terrified by the experience—what does it imply to be face to face with the "All"? He is somewhat disconcerted to realize that this realm is void of concern for morality, ethics, social conscience, or activity of any sort. It is the realm of pure being, in the sense of "that which is," and has no connection with categories other than its own "thusness." The human, confronting it, stands in awe of the suprahuman, and asks, "May I disregard the familiar categories and enter here without incurring the guilt of selfish unconcern?"

Huxley recommends mescaline for the experience; he sees the need for transcendental experience—through religion, drugs, alcohol, tobacco, whatever—as basic to human nature. He refers to the peyote of the Native American Church as an example of the use of drugs in religious practice.

I do not think mescaline, or any other drug, is required to attain a transcendent level. There is a time of the opening of the spirit, of allowing the *flow* of external "appearance-forms" to penetrate the self in all their internal beauty, so that the inner and outer "being" are one. I once wrote a poem about this, on the occasion of a visit to Westminster Abbey in London. I was swept into the "beauty of the abyss," not only by the magnificent appearance of the church, but by the very drapery spread over the rose window at the time. The experience filled me with a kind of wonder mixed with something akin to terror—how could the commonplace arouse in me such a sense of aesthetic awe?

Is this the Buddha state, something analogous to a drug "turn-on"? If so, what brain drug is involved?

This brings up the age-old question: do some people have an extra infusion of this "drug" (naturally)? Hence are they capable of the heightened experiences of the aesthetic response (to their surroundings) as well as to artistic creation as such? Why do some have the natural capacity for altered states of consciousness and other not?

Kate Speaks in Her Sleep

As Kate drifted off to sleep, she mentioned that she had grown up during the Depression. I pointed out that this was impossible, since she had not even been born yet. She insisted that she was born during the Depression era, and that she had died in 1938, at age ten. She added that her name was Marva Jean Roy, daughter of Gene Roy, a farmer who lived near Tulsa, Oklahoma. She had two brothers, Marvin Delmar, then age twelve, and a younger one, Arvin Alfred, who was called "Fred," because he felt that "Alfred" sounded too sissy. (At this point, I am reminded of my father, who changed his name from Roland Alva to R. A., because he felt his given name was too "sissy.")

Kate added that she didn't know whether or not her father owned the farm, but that it was supposed to go to Marvin Delmar when he grew up. Her teacher was Miss June Ella Hancock, who taught at Red River School, near Tulsa. The students called her "Junella." There were two teachers in this country school. When students were ready for high school, they went to Tulsa. She explained that she had died of polio in 1938. The fever "got her"—she "just cooked." "We lived too far from town to get the doctor. They said I had brain fever because I was so smart for my age. I taught myself to read and I taught my brothers to read."

How might one interpret this detailed and engaging account? Various possibilities come to mind: Everything in the exchange is the product of fantasy, the result of Kate's subconscious mind putting together bits and pieces in a fictitious dream sequence that is spoken out as dialogue. There is, in fact, a "spirit" speaking through Kate, someone who experienced the events that she relates. This is indeed Kate's "past self" who is speaking.

An Old Woman Flying

Always now, when I think of myself, it is as an old woman riding the wind, hair flying.

All around me there is a sense of falling space, time dissolving like bubbles. Who knows what minute will be our last, what breath the final, ultimate inspiration.

My mind goes swirling off in jets and spirals, unable to hold to the common measure. My students . . . I want to scream at them, shout at them—shake them, toss them, turn them inside out, face them to a mirror, say, here, now, before it is too late, confront the thing you seek so slowly, face what you search for so unwillingly—the naked, unaltered, unadorned, final reality—yourself.

What I did not realize then was that my world would soon explode.

A Golden Haze or Halo

I know you are there, waiting to find me,
to take me in your heavy jaws,
to gulp me like a morsel
or cough me up like
a briar.

For I am covered in thorns.
No, that's not so.
I am slicked over, oiled,
like something disguised
for a celebration.
I have made myself
an easy prey,
something to be quickly swallowed
and digested
or else spat out in disgust.

You keep calling,
I keep looking the other way.
I beg my responsibilities,
my serious obligations.
You hear none of my
protestations,
they are irrelevant, weightless as air.

You sit back on your great haunches,
swish your tail,
make a warning growl in your throat.
I no longer remember how long
you have been there,
when you came.
Each time I scanned the landscape,
you are always what I saw.
Your mane floats like a golden haze or halo
around your unfathomable face.
Now you are pacing again.

Part 2

Union: self United with Self

The power is the Goddess (Devi) Kundalini, or that which is coiled. . . .

According to Indian notions, success (*siddhi*) in Yoga may be the fruit of experiences in many previous lives. Kundalini—must be gradually raised from one center to another until she reaches the Lotus in the cerebrum. The length of time required varies with the individual—it may be years ordinarily or in exceptional cases months.

In theology this Pure Consciousness is Siva, and His Power (Sakti) who as She is in Her formless self is one with Him. She is the great Devi, the Mother of the Universe who as the Life-Force resides in man's body at the base of the spine just as Siva is realized in the higher brain center, the cerebrum, or Sahasrara-Padma. Completed Yoga is the Union of Her and Him in the body of the Sadhaka. . . .

Arthur Avalon, *The Serpent Power*

It was about to happen. Even before anything was said, I sensed the impending arrival of some event, some occurrence so dramatic, so traumatic that it would unalterably change my life. Once more, I would be cast into the maelstrom of betrayal and confusion. Once again, my relationship would crumble, and I would be dashed against the barriers of the unthinkable, only this time I would be flung through, projected into an unknown sphere of being.

My mind and senses were fully aroused. To quell my rising panic, I continued to write—but not about my personal apprehension, for a direct confrontation with my inner fear was far too intimidating. Rather, I wrote obliquely, focusing on ideas and abstractions—mental discoveries that were flooding my perturbed psyche. By now, Kate and I had been together some ten years. I had come to take for granted the sanctity and security of the relationship. We were living in the same university town, where I had helped to create one of the first women's studies departments in the country, and where Kate was now a graduate student in psychology. Then in mid-May, Kate announced that she wished to go outside our relationship, to explore new avenues with one of her professors (male). I was devastated by this news.

Certainly, I could not stand in her way, for, despite our intimacy on so many levels, what she proposed was something essential to her growth (she obviously needed to experience relationships with others). But I was unprepared for what she proposed. Having held nothing back, I was now completely vulnerable. Once more, my expectations for a permanent, exclusive union were dashed. Once more, I felt I had played love's fool, expecting too much, demanding too little. I stood back, and let the events take their own course. But inwardly, I died. I do not mean this as a metaphor. I experienced acute pain, both psychological and physical, as if my subtle body were under assault. I could hardly bear to maintain consciousness, so threatening were the events unfolding around me. I resigned myself to loss, to the deprivation of that which was most sacred and most meaningful in my life.

After a few days of this agony, I saw a therapist who was also a friend (a heterosexual, she was accepting of other lifestyles). I explained to her what had happened, and said that I would not fear physical death in the future, since it surely would not be as painful as what I was undergoing. She offered some useful insights, and I began to feel somewhat better, for I realized that separation from such a deeply bonded union would also be in some ways liberating for me. For, in truth, we had merged well beyond the limits of what the psyche can reasonably bear. My spirits began to lift.

This was the context in which the crucial events of May unfolded. The entries that follow are from that time, beginning with mental reflections suffused with a sense of underlying turmoil. My background was literature, and now I seemed to read new meanings into familiar texts. For me, these insights were of extreme importance. These were, in fact, the last of the "mental excursions" for some time to come, for the mind was about to "drop" in favor of a different way of knowing.

After this initial period of pain, the experience erupted in a cataclysmic awakening of the energies within. From that point on, my primary relation became the inner, rather than the outer, lover. . . .

Preparing to Greet the Goddess

Do not think of her
unless you are prepared
to be driven to your limits,
to rush forth from yourself
like a ritual bowl overflowing
with sacramental wine.

Do not summon her image
unless you are ready to be blinded,
to stand in the flash

of a center exploding,
yourself shattering into the landscape,
wavering bits of bark and water.

Do not speak her name
until you have said good-bye
to all your familiar trinkets—
your mirrors, your bracelets,
your childhood adorations—
From now on you are nothing,
a ghost sighing at the window,
a voice singing under water.

In the Interval between Each Heartbeat

Row, row, row your boat
Gently down the stream.
Merrily, merrily, merrily, merrily,
Life is but a dream.

Here is another of childhood's rhymes that emerges as wisdom-literature. Consider the motifs and myths here presented: life as journey; the flux as a *stream* (of consciousness, of ever changing appearances, of time); external reality as mere "god-play"; going with the current, like a good Taoist; grace under the pressure of uncertainty.

How is it such illumination comes, as it were, from the mouths of babes? Apparently when sacred texts fail or vanish, then the fundamental truths will be preserved and carried forward through sayings of infants, through legends of childhood. Have not the gods always used such innocents to communicate their truths, to execute their work? So we must listen intently to all that transpires about us, lest the babble conceal a secret profundity.

William I. Thompson speaks of principles of cosmic order that are "programs for the unfolding of being." (At that time I was reading Thompson's *The Time Falling Bodies Take to Light*, a work that deeply influenced my experience.)

I agree. Thus a great or active mind does not so much discover knowledge as allow its inner structure to unfold, automatically embracing the necessary mental configurations at the appropriate junctures. These concepts/thought-trains, in turn, locate and define the mind's own inner process/patterns. Consider: the design of a tree versus the actual, phenomenal tree. Which is the "real" tree?

Into the finite symbol is pressed or compacted that multivalenced meaning that ever stretches toward infinity.

Thompson also says that "in the interval between each thought, in the interval between each heartbeat, in the place where there is no breath, we recall what we always knew."

A Fragment without a Face

W. I. Thompson, in his book *At the Edge of History,* traces the growth of the self as it encounters the many traps and deceptions that Maya presents to us: the illusion of middle class urban West Coast America; the myth of the dream-land (holy Ireland, an image dispelled by coarse reality); the inanities embraced by the hippie dropouts; the superficiality of Esalen; the Byzantine Eastern (seaboard) professors who offer contentions, not truth; the horror of the technological state and its servant-universities.

All this reminds me of an old Abner Dean cartoon from a book called *What Am I Doing Here?* A man, naked and blindfolded, cautiously edges his way forward along the top of a narrow wall, an abyss on either side. Directly in his path, lying along the ridge like animal traps, is a series of "loops" of rope, or inverted nooses, the stem of each hanging over the side, ready to cinch close and drag the walker down if he missteps. Of such drama is our life compounded.

Perhaps the first stage in a safe journey is to realize that we are blind, to know that there are traps before us, to be aware that our expedition is along a precarious margin, one separating the abyss from the abyss.

Or again, do these dead ends and false entry points allegorize the journeyer to paradise who must have the proper answer at each of Heaven's gates or be annihilated on the spot? To succeed, we must unravel (thread by thread if necessary) the blindfold, recognize the noose as another false circle of perfection, and continue our perilous movement forward.

The *Merkabah* rider rips off the blindfold and rushes forward. Blinded by the Sun, too often he falls to right or left, no longer able to maintain the necessary balance. (Certain early kabbalists sought a quick path to God by "riding" a Divine *Merkabah* [God's throne chariot] to Heaven. Often their efforts ended in disaster.)

Here, I drew a diagram based on Yeats' Great Wheel, which is a visual representation of various human personalities and temperaments, each linked to a specific phase of the Moon. In my view, the diagram represented the interrelation of Kate, me, and two others who had played important roles in our lives.

We had connected Kate with phase 13, a deeply sensual phase that can become preoccupied with morbidity when out of sync; her natural complement was Sarah, at phase 27, the martyr, one who, by renouncing personal hopes for salvation, achieves true sanctity. I fell into 17, the phase of Yeats' "demonic man," one passionately seeking contact with the forces of the "other world"; this one also tends to set up idealizations on Earth of the image she carries in her heart, and to suffer numerous disillusionments as a result.

The complement of 17 is 3, the childlike being in tune with nature and all natural life. These paired opposites each strive to attain the level of the other, and thus achieve completion. Together, the four stations form an interconnected unit of being, a "cell of consciousness"; hence the innate attraction of each member for the others.

Consciousness and Reality

Of all external features, that which carries most significance—our own face—is that which we can never see directly. Only by mirrors, water images, photographs, "reflections" can we view the essential signature of our "appearance," the manifestation of visible being by which we announce our presence to the world. Likewise, the inner consciousness, the primary internal register by which we know ourselves, is that which can never be seen by others. For the notion of how we "appear," we must rely on testimony of the external witness (person or reflecting medium). For confirmation of our inner sensibility (for awareness includes the ranges of feeling as well as thought), others must "take our word," as they would our description of a distant or dead friend, one whom they know of but have never met. "I am never so busy as when I do nothing. I am never so accompanied as when I am alone."

This familiar consciousness, then, is always with us (with such obvious exceptions as times of sleep, hallucination, trance, etc.), letting us not forget that we are a fragment without a face (to itself), that the only face we know directly is that of the many-featured world that constantly presents itself to us. Behind the world face, with its highways, its cities, and its creatures, lurks, we suspect, the world soul, the conscious reality we cannot see but whose presence entices us everywhere.

In meditation, consciousness loses itself in stillness. No word mediates experience; we simply are: the light particle suspended in air, the lotus floating on the surface of the lake. We are filled with breath, but not of the body.

A Sphere of Cosmic Energy

Last night—before drifting to sleep—I tried to meditate, and I saw an unusual image of a sphere of light entering a body. The circle invades the body's space (as if the being is pregnant) or the *body* invades the circle's space—it seeks union with energies outside itself. Together they form a symbol: LO.

Now—the body folds itself round the curves of the sphere, and the sphere begins to rotate.

The body is enfolded into motion. The whole is a circular stream whirling about a center (recalling pictures of Earth from outer space, or Blake's mystic spirals).

Then another dimension is added and we have the cyclonic spiral, moving and wavering through space like an animated spring.

I also visualized other archetypal images, including Blake's spirals and Yeats' intertwining cones, plus pictures of rotating Earth taken from space.

Now, in *this* vision, the human *first* existed as an identity in itself, though "pregnant" with the circle/sphere. As the sphere turns, the human is "folded into" it, along the periphery, merging almost totally into the field of rotation. Yet a trace (of the human dimension) remains. The image offers me a glimpse of origins, a *source* for the later manifestations (of the myriad actualized beings of the universe). And a clearer revelation of all of these images as emblems of the human *linked to* the divine, attached but not consumed, drawn along the whirling cosmic path but never fully divested of its inner identity. "Two are one, and yet that one is also itself."

Thus the human is charged with cosmic energies—pulled into, but not absorbed by the form of forms. The suprahuman finds an outlet in the direction, shape, concretion of the human for its yearning for tangible expression, that it may touch, see, know itself in a featured, moving landscape.

I also saw a funnel. At its absolute center is an opening— Yeats' needle's eye, the spurting sperm-fountain of the inverted cornucopia—from which pour forth all the invented forms and tangible realities of the manifest universe.

To be born is to pass through the slit in the vortex. To be caught in the rotation of the fiery wheel is to experience the whole as energy. This is the realm of that which becomes; to step outside and witness both the dreamer and the dream is, possibly, a step toward fuller understanding of the ongoing spectacle.

Clearly, these images were as well foreshadowings of what was about to occur, a fusion of the two levels, human and divine, a baptism of the flesh in the fires of kundalini.

Discovering Lindisfarne

I continued to read the work of William I. Thompson, and was deeply excited by the ideas I found there. The fact that Thompson came from an American academic background seemed to bring closer the whole realm of Eastern thought and practices; meditation, yoga, kundalini—he mentioned all these, and they seemed to lose some of their exotic flavor and enter the realm of possible experience. Thompson himself is a visionary, a poet/prophet of great force and effectiveness. His work, with its potent oracular style, seemed to become the trigger for the experience toward which I was moving.

When I discovered that Thompson's "New Age" association called Lindisfarne (after the ancient English monastery) was located in southern Colorado, I was determined to make contact. It seemed like an incredible opportunity to break out of the isolation in which I had pursued my own studies of the inner life for so many years, and to encounter like-minded, more advanced souls. The following is an excerpt from a letter I never sent. The heightened tone reveals my excited state of mind; the crisis in my personal life had reached a level of mounting, near unbearable intensity, and I turned to Thompson's words in a state of desperation, seizing on them to alleviate my inner turmoil. I had reached what Yeats calls a state of frenzy. All possibilities were now open.

I am a long-time student of many of the systems (thoughts? areas?) you allude to in your writings. I am affiliated with no group, cult, or movement. Certainly, I have no vision or final answers to anything. My instruction is mainly from books (Yeats, D. Lessing, Neumann, Zukov, Blavatsky [who makes no sense at all], Eliade, H. Smith, J. Campbell, Blofeld, Jung, Blake—the lot). I raise no spirits, light no candles. For the most part, it has been a solitary occupation. Sometimes, I feel like the old time "Lone Scout," (I believe this was the term)—the isolated boy caught out on a farm somewhere, who wanted to be a Boy Scout but had no troop or pack to relate to.

Since I have had no one to speak with on these matters, I have of necessity become an "autodidact," in the sense of one who converses primarily with the private self. You have revealed your own inner self with incredible openness in your books.

And for this I salute you—for your courage, your vision, your truths. I hope that a way can be found for me to participate more fully in your movement. I feel I can make a contribution, in whatever capacity or mode.

Three Encounters

My dread, my anxiety, continued to mount. I sensed that something was dreadfully wrong, but as yet I did not know what. I continued to write frantically in my journal, but I could not bear to confront in words the reality of what was about to erupt. Instead, I wrote about literary illustrations of human encounter with larger forces, focusing on the "other" rather than on self. I described "Hamlet as Gnostic Allegory" (spirit versus flesh). Then I interpreted "Ahab versus the Archon" (the fury of the enfleshed mortal set against the invisible omnipotent). And I reflected upon "Oedipus and His Victim" (the disaster of impulsive action.) I concluded:

Here, then, are three versions of encounter—masculine, fatal, clustering about the poles of enlightenment (whence come I?) and power (O, what is man, that thou art mindful of him?). In each, self is posed against the Other. Perhaps there is another mode, the path of love as caritas/eros, to take us through the rounds of self to self.

But the appalling revelation of *eros* is that it thrives not on gratitude but gratification. We can act with total honor, give until we are impoverished, bend our wishes to the other's every whim—but still, love may be denied, or be only temporarily bestowed, departing on its own signal.

Love and justice have nothing in common. *Eros* breeds joy and pain equally, thrives best in situations of disequilibrium. The path of *caritas* is a chilly one. But perhaps it is the only path to final redemption. And how desolate is the spirit when it takes its first upward step.

All Things Turn into Their Opposites

What I dreaded had come about. Once again I was confronted by the loss of what I most valued, but I was far too devastated to speak openly of my agony. I confided in no one. I simply

surrendered to events, and underwent a deep, indeed excruciating, inner death. In a state of mental and physical anguish, I continued my exploration of abstractions, ideas suggested by the
specifics of the inner crisis.

I realized at a deep level that all things turn constantly into
their opposites. Thus, even at the very beginning of love, the
beloved is moving away from us, into the realm of the undesir-
able/unattainable.

And I reflected on the deceptive nature of the false ego self.

A Movie Projector

Consider a machine, a movie projector. Into it a film strip is
threaded—something to be drawn by hand across the face of the
machine. Now, it (the device) observes, and says of what it sees, "I
am this." On the film, events occur in time. Faces move from youth
to age, bodies gather the weight of the years. There is emotion,
grief, tears. There is fear, loss, achievement. The gadget watches
itself, learns some few lessons, gathers insights. At the end it
repeats (tells) the lesson it has learned. If it is successful, it goes on
to a new film, a new "story of 'I.'" If it fails, then it must repeat—
endlessly, perhaps—the enactment of the same basic scenario.

The machine—the self—is outside of time, space, or *personality*. It is *pure consciousness*, without definition.

We (the players) all look at the same world. But for each, one
essential element is missing—ourselves. Our own face is what we
can never see directly. Our task is to fathom its features as best
we can from indirection, reflection, hints, and clues. Perhaps
this is the face we had before we were born.

We are author, actor, and critic of the individual drama. Out of
a spaceless/timeless world we learn through events enacted on the
time-bound, space-oriented stage. If we knew it was only a stage, we
would be insufficiently *in* the drama to experience it. If we merely
acted and did not observe, we would never move to illumination.

Constantly we go forth from the One (which is undifferenti-
ated) into the state of the Other, which is the self seen in its dis-

tinction from the source. (From the point of view of the self, the *One* is other.)

The Task of the Lover

From the Inner Voice: This is one of the most painful and potentially rewarding of all paths. It is a high risk venture. Like the figure of the *Merkabah* (throne chariot) rider, the soul may leap instantaneously into heaven or be totally annihilated.

The danger is that the soul will fasten on the beloved in its material manifestation—the body, the personality—and fail to grasp the underlying significance of the event.

The soul is opened up through love. Every experience becomes more intense, more sensory, sensual, emotional. This prepares the mind to open, to pierce the veil of illusion, or, rather, to allow the outer to become inner, the impulse to manifest as perception.

The ultimate aim is to still the soul. By agitation, tumult, even frenzy—to come to a still place, proof against all distress. Until this stage is successfully passed, there can be no movement on to the path of the sage.

Perhaps the lovers write a common script beforehand, in order to help one another. Bargains are struck, promises made. Each seeks to obtain that lesson it needs.

Conditions for the Journey

A compelling attraction. One answers some need in the other. One fulfills some lack, some necessity. Psychological. Emotional. Even material. "You offer what I seek and must have for completion. I am *compelled* to merge with you."

The love is set at the center of the stage. All other subplots—work, fame, friendship, social involvement—are secondary.

In this heat, two souls are literally burned together, fused into a single psychic identity. This singleness then wars within itself, struggling to be free, a unique being once again. The souls separate, and bring out of the experience what they have gained there-from—pain and passion turned to awareness.

If this stage is passed successfully, it results in a major initiation.

The Laws of this Relation

There will be no rest—the lovers will be constantly propelled forward, either by ecstasy or despair.

The intensity must be maintained. The lovers may exhaust themselves in the dance, but then they must rise to dance again.

There will be many masks—and masks beneath masks. There will be no final unmasking.

All the symbols will activate.

Kate says that our "goal" is the integration of the four levels—spiritual and emotional, mental and physical; that our "purpose" is to achieve the integration that will prepare us for our assigned task, or else the integration is itself the task.

Union

By now, my spirit had confronted its ultimate terror. The ideal love relation, the mythology that had supported it, the sense of unassailable trust—all had been shattered irrevocably.

But, in the midst of such emotional devastation, some small seed of hope was beginning to stir. For loss also brings with it freedom, the unleashing of the self to pursue its own destined ends, to find its own inner reality. The inner death had prepared an opening.

On this sunny morning, I sat quietly in my living room, writing in my journal. My elm-lined street carried little sound other than the drone of an occasional passing car. It was spring; the trees were already heavy with green, and the flowers were coming to bloom along this typical midwestern city street. I was contemplating the notion of balances, the desired midpoint between.

And then, I was awakened.

The book I was reading mentioned kundalini but did not describe it in detail. It spoke of the ancient yogis who could raise the "serpent power" from the base of the spine to the head. On impulse, I decided to see if I could lift my own energies this way. I meditated on an image of the god and goddess in union (Shiva/Shakti from an illustration in the text) and focused on my breathing. Almost instantaneously I felt a great surge of ecstatic energy in the lower charkas and then, within seconds, this intense force rushed upward and into my head. My very crown seemed to open in rapture, and for many minutes, I felt the energies of the unseen immensity flow in, as if petal after radiant petal were unfolding in my crown. As long as I did not think about what was happening, the experience continued, but each time self-awareness intruded, the process was interrupted.

In that moment of grace, I realized that the notion of personal identity was an ongoing illusion, a myth the small being recites to itself in its state of lostness and isolation. I knew that we were each one but atoms within the larger frame, the boundless real. . . . I did not return immediately to ordinary consciousness. I remained in a state of exalted awareness and rapture for months thereafter. I seemed to undergo a prolonged initiation directed by unseen guides. I saw the light around my body and heard my new name. I experienced deep rapture each time I called up the image of the god/goddess in union. Even when I was not meditating, I was filled with strong, ecstatic energies.

During this time I "discovered" certain "initiatory" implements, such as a tiny bell, a vajra (for me, a crystal prism in the shape of a barbell) and a design I thought of as a yantra (an image for meditation). With these instruments and with much inner guidance I completed a major weeklong initiation. On the final day I saw in a vision an inner image of Christ on the cross.

The world was now lit by an inner beauty surpassing everything I had experienced before, as if I saw the beauty beneath the beauty. Every face was my own, every leaf or bloom an aspect of my being. I felt that I had, at last, fused all levels; I knew, finally and incontrovertibly, that spirit and flesh are one, matter and the transcendent but different faces of a single essence.

Brain and Base

What led up to this experience?

First, there was the fever pitch writing of last summer. I felt as though I *had* to extract and formulate certain basic ideas that were fundamental to any complete understanding of reality. The course I taught last fall, with its emphasis on masculine-feminine principles in literature, was also important. (It included everything from D. H. Lawrence to Nor Hall.) Then there were the two negative encounters—two people, each of whom attempted to make me a "victim."

One was a young man in the class, a self-proclaimed fundamentalist, who challenged everything I said, yet tried to find a mystical bond between us. I was quite frightened of him, particularly when he insisted that the "androgynous Christ" was a fraud, and that only the literal interpretation of the Bible was true. Something about him seemed disturbed and even threatening. The other challenge had to do with one of my female colleagues who, rightly or wrongly, was incensed at one of my administrative decisions (made in consultation with a committee), and attacked me with vehement letters to other colleagues and administrators.

The emotions aroused by the first incident had subsided once the semester was over and I no longer had to face a daily encounter with an intimidating presence. As for my colleague, I felt that I doubtless had wronged her, and despite the hostile nature of her response, I should respond to her with love, no matter what. She confessed that she also had been disturbed both emotionally and physically by what had happened, and we were now proceeding as friends, not enemies. Both of these were intense, emotional experiences, in which I confronted my innate tendency to cast myself as another's victim. The lesson of each encounter seemed to be to find a way to avoid the victim trap.

What I experienced yesterday was, I think, a foretaste of nirvana in samsara. I took powerful, sweet energy into the head, and experienced what Thompson calls a "sexualized brain," and a "conscious" body. The feelings were strong and intense. The main centers affected were the brain and the sexual centers. Are these the second and sixth chakras? According to Thompson, this is a male pattern. He says that women's energies naturally flow from lower centers to the heart, while men must *learn* to bring energies out of the head to the heart. Well, possibly I do conform to a male pattern, and possibly this is no surprise. In any event, *all* of the pelvic area and *all* of the brain area were involved. I was aware of little feeling in the throat, chest, or navel.

The energies seemed to leap from lower to higher centers and then flow ecstatically back and forth. I felt that Shiva had indeed united with Shakti, that energy *outside my head* (the energy of everything that is) flowed into my skull, flooding my being with delight. The experience lasted for as long as I did not think about what I was doing. Each time I became "self-conscious," the sensations diminished. I finally quit of my own accord, thinking it best not to continue too long.

Inner Counsel

In a state of continuing rapture and light trance, I asked my guides for direction, particularly for help in dealing with the intensity of the energies:

Q. Is there a "day-to-day" meditation—to get us through when we are not eager for higher, more intense forms?

A. The student should choose the form of meditation she is comfortable with. Certainly it is unwise to *press for* intensity. *Allow* your body/being to receive its proper due. You can be happy only with the right proportion. Too little/too much destroy balance and set up either hunger or despair.

Q. How far does one go on one's own?

A. As far as one is comfortable with.

Q. Life seems to flow in oscillations of death/rebirth sequences. Does the final oscillation carry us into death?

A. Yes. In life the swing of emotions passes through ever-widening arcs until it finds a point of balance at the center. We experience repetitions of various stages of experience, always with greater intensity. The final recapitulation sweeps us to death.

Q. Why does the West reject the body? Why do Plato and Christianity reject not only the *body* but all it implies—nature, woman, the feminine principle, feeling—and thus repudiate possibilities of oneness, integration, and completion?

A. Fear. Without balance, body overturns the soul. Better a soul without a body than a body without a soul. Better a higher without a lower than a lower without a higher.

Q. Why does my hand hurt a little now?

A. Again, fear. Fear of losing touch with the human, fear of the isolation you knew before human love broke in, of losing Kate's love and your love for her, sadness at the passing of time, of moving to a new phase.

Three Precepts:

1. Be satisfied with the level of attainment.
2. Be open to progress in attainment.
3. Remember that the path/way is the goal.

The Two Initiations

In this experience, as in all such experiences, an outer is combined with an inner source (that is, part of the awakening *seems* to come from an external stimulus). I have now undergone two separate initiations, in *two* systems. The first (orchestrated by M. Kabal, our "kabbalistic" inner guide), was, of course, terminated as not achieving its intended goals, though it was not entirely unsuccessful.

Comparison of the two experiences:

- Both used what was startling to capture our attention. The first used the Ouija board itself, inner lights, a vision of patriarchs coming from heaven. The second utilized the opening of the chakras. The former path, with its accompanying psychic manifestations, was too threatening.

- Both involved an opening to new, profound insights. In the former, there were many "unusual occurrences," essentially occult in nature. The present experience arouses a sense of the oneness and beauty of all creation.

- The first awakened fear, a sense of inner disturbance, being shaken out of one's center. The second was suffused with joy, a sense of unity and oneness with all things, a feeling of being grounded: "I am myself only different."

Transcendent Bliss

Again, I try to describe my present state of being. I am too far gone in altered consciousness to produce a flowing narrative account. I am reduced to merely cataloging the essentials.

How I characterize what I now feel:

- Transcendent bliss—experienced as pleasure in the brain.

- Total unitive consciousness of all levels of myself—(but this awareness is not continuous in time).

- Acceptance of the dissolution of the karmic bond between Kate and me.

- A "stirring" of the brain through meditation.

- A deep sense of the beauty underlying the beauty of the trivial, the everyday, the ordinary. A sense of the "oneness" of subject and object.

- A feeling as if the chakras had opened and the higher mingled with the lower to reach an elevated state of consciousness.

- The deep security of knowing that what is within is still within, it will be there.

- A wish to *go forward,* to Lindisfarne and all that it implies.

- Some nostalgia for all that has transpired between us (Kate and me).

- A sense of an experience that is totally new yet not unfamiliar.

- A sense of reaching a certain *level* of enlightenment (one that I can deal with).

Whatever the future holds, it now contains an element that was not present before: a reality, an actuality, which was before only potential.

Q. How can two lovers dissolve a karmic bond and yet
    1. Still be lovers on Earth?
    2. Still be together in the interim?

A. 1. By way of nonpossession, to love and not possess, to allow the other to fulfill her nature.
    2. Because they are part of the same oneness.

The Stages of Transformation

I continued to try to understand this experience in terms of conventional stages of initiation and transformation:

Initiation into all systems is ever the same—whether it be Kaballah, alchemy, a Christian vision, even Tarot meditation. First, there is a signal, a sign, a "startling into awareness." This brings the cracking of the old soul, the dissolution of the "old Adam," by fire, erosion, revelation. The result is disunity—the dissolution of the old self. There is deep disturbance as the dark night of the soul closes in, bringing death of the old being. The soul grieves its loss, and the subtle body is torn. At last there is a coming to terms, experienced as a willingness to "let go" and allow transformation to occur. One senses a "balancing out" of the being. There must be a "willing surrender" of the prior self—an intense but "comfortable" openness to the new experience.

What follows must be something startling yet familiar, a realization of what has been longed for as image, an actualization of a keen desire.

The initiate must be jolted but not overwhelmed. She should recognize that what has happened is an intensification and expansion of her essential self.

Thus occurs the "opening of the chakras," the baptism by fire. A spirit guide may appear. The scales may fall and reveal "signs and wonders."

Now comes a sense of election, of revelation, and the unexpected discovery of the New Self begotten through a new experience.

If the initiate be "balanced" (in phase, at one with self and others), the effect is to propel her forward to a new path, which is the old path recognized at last. She will experience deep feelings of oneness and love for all that is, and note with awe the "beauty beneath the beauty" of the manifest universe. Her happiness will be extreme, for this is the home she has sought so long. And she will hurry to consolidate her instruction so that others may join in this communion.

Finally, one moves through ecstasy into unitive consciousness in which the world reveals its underlying beauty and the many facets of self are fused at a higher level than any known before.

Energy is the key to everything. Solar and lunar, head and loins, beast, atom, stars. Everything issues from and turns upon the same source. But this source cannot be truly defined: "Man can embody truth but not know it" (Yeats).

Prana in the head—this is the state of being blessed in *both* body and soul.

I now considered the many kinds of ecstasy I had experienced in my lifetime, in order to see how personal experience related to universal experience. I thought of the intense delight of the child in the world of nature; experiences of love as an adult; visits to sacred places (Ireland, Lascaux, Eleusis, Delphi, the Rocky Mountains near Boulder, Colorado, the countryside near Innsbruck, Austria). I thought of the teacher who introduced me to Emerson, Wordsworth, and The Church of Christ, Scientist, when I was sixteen, young enough to experience a classic spiritual conversion into a world full of transcendent love and beauty. And, of course, I reviewed my experience with M. Kabal, who led me into frenzy.

Two or three nights ago I dreamed that there was something in my eye, such as two or three little eyelashes. In the dream, it is important that it is the *left* eye. Evelyn Underhill, in her *Mysticism*, quotes *Theologica Germanica* as follows:

> The two eyes of the soul of man cannot both perform their work at once: but if the soul shall see with the right eye into eternity, then the left eye must close itself and refrain from working, and be as though it were dead. For if the left eye be fulfilling its office toward outward things; that is, holding converse with time and the creatures; then must the right eye be hindered in its working; that is, in its contemplation. Therefore, whosoever will have the one must let the other go; for "no man can serve two masters."

The interpretation is clear.

The Riddle of Infinity

Infinity is two zeros lying on their side. Everything that is and everything that is not. What is in the cave, unborn, and what is out, the manifest. Reality before and after. The nothingness of before the beginning—the nothingness after the end.

This is why scientists cannot solve the riddle of infinity in space. There is no "space"; there is only idea. What are the physical boundaries of a dream? Does it end at a spatial limit of itself? Or simply turn into something else? A dream has no space, nor is its "time" our own.

If the scientists would relent, accept the notion that the world is a kind of thought or emanation of mind, they would attain a new understanding of the universe.

Yantra Meditation

Now I spent time meditating on a sacred design, which I thought of as my yantra. Yantra meditation (prolonged concentration on a sacred image or geometric form) is said to be one of the most difficult exercises in tantric practice. It typically takes the student years to learn to follow and experience internally the energies awakened by the emblem. For me, the inner response—sweet flowing bliss in the head—was instantaneous.

My yantra was actually a luminous decal intended for a window. Called "Flower of Truth," it consisted of an arabesque (a design of tangled vines) containing four arrows coming from the four directions, all pointing to a star in the center. At the bottom appeared these words: "The simple flower of truth exists within the web of illusion. Arrows from the four directions point the way from outer entanglements to the cool peace at the center." As I gazed, I perceived even more images within the swirling mesh.

At the center was a star with eight sides. Looking fixedly, I saw the star become the jagged form of the "circle saw" that I have so often drawn or sketched almost unconsciously. After a few more moments of meditation, I beheld two heads joined back to back, which I identified as Kate and me.

The four arrows, coming from the four directions, represented (for me) the four persons—Kate, me, and the two others with whom we were connected through the typology of Yeats'

Great Wheel, which I reviewed once more. The four arrows also suggested the four "levels" of body, emotion, mind, and spirit.

I then saw two crossed *vajras* (sacred Tibetan implements resembling wands with bulbs on each end). These signified the head-base union (if you can make these opposites merge, you can merge all else).

So I continued to gaze at the cross-pattern of this:

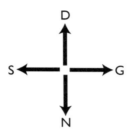

As I looked at the center, the arrows of the four directions seemed to press into and through me. Energies formed and I felt the "throb of bliss" following the path of each arrow in the head. I repeated the sensation for a few minutes—and was content.

I find this an easy way to meditate, to experience the energies. This is delightful, safe, natural, good. It is a *releasing* of inner energy (imagery), for they are the same.

Now everything seems to fall into place.

The Light around the Body

Seven years ago, when I experienced the "incomplete initiation" in Boulder, I looked in the mirror and saw my face transformed (I thought) into a demon. I was crushed. I felt defeated, a failure. I had sought a "spiritual" (i. e., nonbody) symbol as my confirmation. What I got was the satyr-goat. With a deep sense of humility, I interpreted the symbol as "the mask of Silenus—your father and your guide." I discovered that Silenus was the teacher of Dionysus, who leads us through ecstasy to wisdom. And I have indeed learned *all* from Silenus—from ecstasy.

Now I go again to the mirror, this time in a state of heightened pleasure. I see the light around the body. An inner voice repeats: "Bodhidharma, filled with light." I see my mouth *move* and I realize that my task is to be a "truth-speaker" (my interpretation of this title). I watch many versions of my face appear and dissolve, all variations of my present self except one. This is the image of my friend with whom I had had the misunderstanding a few weeks ago. She is now my "twin," her face gazing at me from the reflected image, but she looks angry, mean-spirited, someone filled with bitterness. I realize that here is unfinished business, that I must bathe her in love, for there is a bond between us; indeed, I am she, as I am all. I see only a few of these connections now, but I know I must start with these and open toward others.

I perform a few graceful gestures of my own devising and feel the sweet energy flow through my body. Then I walk a bit with the bell that I had used in my initiation, and again sense the energies moving.

Thus, we start with a desperate need to see our face, but at the end, when it is time to look, we are not interested, for *we* are the others. They are the ones we look toward and *are*. *We* have a form, a point about which an identity collects, so that others can relate to us. We had no face before we were born. We are all faces.

Only when ego no longer exists can ego attain its goals.

What is trapped in the merely human can only exist on the mundane level. Transcendence of self moves us to another plane where Heaven and Earth mingle.

Now I see that by rejecting the physical, I could not attain the spiritual. By embracing the physical, I am led to the spiritual. In ecstasy, we become energy. This energy we use to transform (serve) others.

For now, I want no more words—only *images* to unite with.

The Crown of a King, Christ on the Cross

This morning McGuire, the sheepdog, did something quite unusual. She refused to go out into the backyard. Just now, I tried again, and she refused, so I took her to the front, and sat on the step to wait. After a few minutes, she came close to me, wanting to be loved. Then she did something she has *never* done before. She took me into the house by pulling at my arm with her foot. She pulled me up and into the house. Was she guarding me? Was she ill? Was she afraid of the wasps that had collected about the house? In any event, she accomplished the goal of getting me back indoors when I was thinking that the events of the day had been concluded.

Once in the house, I sat quietly, and internal images immediately arose. I had the sense that this was a "final" session. In part, it was a review of what I planned to do with this newfound energy, how I would respond to people at large, to Kate. In part it consisted of messages which I understood that I would not remember. I asked if it had been the crown chakra that had opened in my head. I received an image of a king (like the king in alchemy) wearing a crown. I was the king, much to my surprise. Then came another inner vision of Christ on the Cross, Christ the Healer. I sensed how he took the pain of others into himself, and how much they needed this. As I contemplated this image, I *felt* pain along my arms, legs, and other places. Then I received instruction on how to handle pain in healing by "transforming it into joy." As I thought these words, I felt joy return to my limbs.

This is like a current of energy that one controls mentally by *allowing* (wishing, desiring) it to happen. It is like a sixth sense that functions in ways similar to the other senses. Thus, one has some control of vision in that one opens the eyes to see, but the eyes do the seeing. Likewise, one *turns* to hear better, but one cannot will the ears to hear. One wishes the energy to manifest, but one does not control its subsequent expression.

And now—the sixth sense is a sense of joy, deriving from a truly "altered consciousness."

Thus the week of deep initiation came to its close. The effects would, however, dramatically alter everything in my subsequent life.

I discovered that I had, intuitively, incorporated many of the stages of a "first-level" Buddhist empowerment initiation into my inner drama, including the ablution (showering became an important rite for me throughout the week), holding the sacred implements (vajra and bell), receiving my new name, and wearing the crown—this last effect achieved through the answer to my final question on the last day. In addition, I had included elements of tantric practice, such as the meditation on the god and the goddess embracing, and contemplation of the yantra.

Clearly, there was orchestration from an inner guide or guides—indeed, the entire sequence, seen in retrospect, appeared to have been timed to occur at this very critical juncture of overwhelming ego loss through a crisis that had been in preparation for many years. To gain what I most treasured (divine love as palpable presence) I was forced to surrender that which I most treasured (human love at the center of my life).

Yoga Pleasure

On this morning, I attempted yoga asanas for the first time ever. I had no real book of instruction, only a small text illustrated with simple drawings. With this basic introduction, I assumed the various postures and discovered, to my amazement, that each position produced its own flow of ecstatic energies. I thought to myself, "No wonder people do yoga. It produces bliss with virtually no effort." Clearly, I was still in a state of rapturous trance rather than rational awareness.

What do I make of such statements as this, that kundalini rises only for the student after long practice? Or that only great masters can meditate from a mental image (picture)? Or that, for women, the energy follows a path connecting womb and breast?

On Friday, I quickly grasped the yantra technique and felt much pleasure in the head. There was much stirring about in the brain, much delight under the skull. Perhaps the male takes semen into the brain (as the ancient texts proclaim), and the female takes ecstasy into the head. Phase 17 on Yeats' Wheel (with which I have identified) is the station of "simplification (purification) through intensity," an apt description of this experience.

As I performed the *asanas* I felt intense energetic pleasure in every limb. Each movement, even the lifting of an arm or leg, aroused exquisite sensations within. The body was indeed what I had to claim, and this is what I do now through this exercise (yoga) and this meditation *(yantra)*.

But I long for something gentler to live with. I do not wish to experience a full kundalini rising each time; it is too powerful, too overwhelming. And there are other negative aspects to the experience. I was most uncomfortable going out to dinner Friday evening. Being in a room full of people and noise created great chaos and confusion within. When I went to bed Friday night, I could not turn the current off. It became a source of dismay, not joy. I woke about 3 A.M. with a terrible pain in my coccyx, which has been sore off and on for two or three years. I couldn't get back to sleep. Internal lights may have been flashing. I got up and stayed up till dawn.

Light Streams from Buddha's Eyes

This morning, I woke quite early. I had a mental image of Buddha, with streams of light flowing from his eyes into a pool before him. A voice (inner) said: "Light streams from Buddha's eyes into the water." This, I understood, was the stream of things manifesting, the flood of particularization, of many-ness. Ultimately, it will all return to him. The water was not an ocean, but an enclosed pool with specific boundaries. It reminded me of biblical stories of the creation, God moving over the waters. It also made me remember a dream I had two months ago, in which I journeyed and journeyed, always west, until I came to a place in the mountains. This place had people (unidentified) connected with it, and also several buildings, not collected into a village, but scattered about, almost at random. The buildings were associated, yet they were not combined in a single community. There was also a lake or man-made pool. It was significant that it was an artificial lake, not natural. I was overjoyed to arrive there. I recognized it as the place I had been seeking, my spiritual destination.

About the same time, I had another dream, this one clearly predictive of the future. In this dream, Kate left me, but at the same time she was still with me, physically present. I was not disturbed in the dream, and I thought this bespoke a reassuring inner confidence.

A Class for the Future

I do well at the women's studies office in the mornings. *(Because it was summer, I was now working only half days as director.)* But by afternoon, I feel a rising anxiety, even though I go home at noon. This anxiety can be tiring. Also, I seem to internalize and share the pain of certain disturbed people. It seems to be much easier to assimilate within myself than to integrate the new self with the outer world.

Today I designed a "futurist" course. I want to have the students very active in the course; they will do yoga, meditation, tai chi; there will be sections on the critical state of the Earth at present, the utopias of the past, and the entry into a Sacred Way through new visions of the Body, Earth, Mind, and Spirit. Topics would range from holistic medicine to new physics to the art of the emerging era.

In fact, I did succeed in teaching this class, or one similar to it, several times in the coming years. I slipped it into the curriculum of one of the most conservative, hidebound, anti–New Age universities in the country, one set squarely at the center of Middle America, where things, especially ideas, seldom change. But students hungry for the new learning came eagerly to the class. For many, it was their first opportunity to share dramatic personal experience with others, and to discover how the pattern of their individual lives fit into what was happening throughout society.

I was surprised to discover how many of these (mostly women in their thirties or early forties) had experienced near-death or out-of-body experiences, and what a deep spiritual impact these encounters had had on their lives. Although the institution was in many ways an anachronism, the students (and a few select faculty) were not. These students were seeking the best of both traditional learning and the new awareness. We saw clearly that the future does not discard the past. Rather it gathers it into itself and carries it upward to a new level of the ongoing spiral.

Bhagwan's Truth

Fortunately for me, the friend-therapist I visited when the crisis unfolded in my life was a follower of Bhagwan Shree Rajneesh. When I related my experience to her, she accepted it as "normal" behavior, and even confirmed that what I had experienced was a form of "ecstasy."

Today, Ann lent me her book called *Meditation: The Art of Ecstasy.* I was surprised to discover in Bhagwan's writings various parallels with my own reflections and experiences. He asserts that the last image before the mind dissolves will be the spiritual figure most deeply embedded in the psyche of the initiate, a symbol drawn from the original religion. Hence, my "last image" of Christ on the cross. He also utilizes the metaphor of the projector as a device for the display of ego. He says that we must wait, maybe, a lifetime for illumination. He discusses being and nothingness, each of which calls the other "reality."

As for Bhagwan, I find his phoniness, his commercialism, and his charismatic posturing all extremely distasteful. Yet I agree with everything he says in this book.

Although I sensed the presence of many guides during the week of my inner initiation, only one took clear shape in my mind, and he only flitted across my consciousness a couple of times. He seemed to be a young man in his late thirties, well built, sturdy, almost robust, in peak physical condition. He wore a leather vest, no shirt, possibly a headband. This "hippie guide" may have been in charge of the whole procedure. He was perfectly poised, confident in what he was doing. (I connect him with the "karate expert" of my amyl nitrate vision, the man of surging physical energy.)

I wrote Ann a note and gave it to her at the end of our session: "Yes, I did go to the very verge of madness. Yes, I did pull back barely in time. Yes, I did die and accept initiation. Yes, I will continue since there is nothing to return to."

A good therapist, she merely smiled and gave me a reassuring hug.

Today, I felt much ecstasy all day, including this afternoon while I did asanas.

I continue to change my habits: my diet is much lighter now, mostly fruits and vegetables, and I have given up smoking.

Life Review

Once more, I reviewed the sequence of my life, with its seven-year cycles of transition. I noted that this most recent and most important change in my life had occurred at the age of fifty-three, fourteen years after the move to Kansas. I observed that my life would probably suffer another major shift when I was sixty. (This prediction proved to be correct, for when I reached sixty, I retired from my university position and moved to San Francisco.)

I thought also once more of the recurring leitmotif *in my life, that of deep love followed by what (for me) seemed like abandonment and betrayal. I thought of the many years I had spent grieving for lost love, and how suffering had more than once brought me close to nervous collapse. Each time, I clung to my suffering like a treasure.*

It was primarily because of this perpetual clinging to lost love, this incessant need to martyr myself for another, that I identified so strongly with the seventeenth phase of Yeats' Great Wheel. In A Vision, *Yeats says of this personality:*

> The *Body of Fate*, therefore, derived from a phase of renunciation, is "loss," and works to make impossible

"simplification by intensity." The being, through the intellect, selects some object of desire . . . as Image, some woman perhaps, and the *Body of Fate* snatches away the object. Then the intellect . . . must substitute some new image of desire; and . . . relate that which is lost to the new image of desire. . . . It will feel itself betrayed, and persecuted.

Obviously, in my earlier years, I was "out of phase," for when I experienced loss, I was always devastated, and felt myself "betrayed and persecuted" until I found a new object of love to adore. More recently, the period of mourning seemed to shorten somewhat, and the recovery to become a little easier. This time, the "death of the spirit" had been (essentially) compressed into a few excruciating days, and recovery had brought an introduction into a new way of being.

A Repeated Pattern

This experience, like that of the psychic awakening of seven years ago, involves a similar pattern of precipitating events. It begins with an activation of the "male principle" in the lives of both Kate and me. For me, the principle emerges as a young man in my class who discovers a mysterious connection between himself and me. In 1974, it was T., who was deeply disturbed. He spoke in tongues, and believed he was the reincarnation of a Nazi SS trooper. He wanted my picture to send to his psychic adviser, but I was uneasy with this idea. He was a very sweet boy, but the Ouija warned against him.

At the first session when T. and others were present (before we found M. Kabal as our contact—he later told us he had attended this session, but "did not control the planchette"), the entire evening produced only gibberish and garbled messages. But when I examined the notes carefully next day, I found one intelligible but disturbing passage: "How do you know T. is T.?" I was frightened by the thought that T. might be "possessed," or whatever, and kept my distance from him from that time on.

This time around, the young man was the lone male in my women's literature class. He was, he explained to me, an ex-Marine and a virgin. He was also a fundamentalist Christian who wrote virulent papers on witches, a subject he had selected for himself (obviously, he hated or feared women at a very deep level). He felt there was some special connection between himself and me. I was frankly intimidated by him—something about him seemed even sinister. So, as with T., I kept my distance. But each episode served to focus my attention squarely on a male, and on my relationship with him.

For Kate, the male principle activates as a male professor she is fascinated with (it is the same professor each time). Seven years ago, the relationship was not actually consummated. But this time it was, at least briefly, and thus it became the impetus for my own deep inner experience.

Recently, this man came to my office and asked if I would "forgive" him for what he had done. I assured him that I held no grudge, and gave him a hug. And indeed, I feel no animosity toward him. Kate was obviously intent on playing out this drama. I think I might as well have tried to stop a tornado as to prevent this from occurring. It seemed to be something which simply "had to happen." Actually, I felt a strange bond with him.

New Age Culture and Women's Studies

My primary professional interest for many years had been women's studies. I had helped to create the program at my university in the early 1970s, and had served as its coordinator since that time. Now I was looking for ways to introduce ideas of the new consciousness into the curriculum. My own experience had clearly arisen after years of focus on the balancing of the male/female energies, and from a willingness to open to the "feminine principle," by which one is endowed with a new state of being, rather than attempting to shape events through masculine, aggressive modes. My dean (who had been consistently supportive of women's studies) encouraged me to apply for travel funds to attend a conference at the Lindisfarne Center in Colorado. Here is the memo I sent as an official rationale for the requested funds.

What Do the New Consciousness and Women's Studies Have in Common?

- Both recognize the need for social restructuring, but emphasize a process of *inward transformation* as prerequisite for external reform.

- Both rely on the capacity of the "product" (the person) to change the process (society) by which the creature has been created.

- Both assume that "human values" are in fact "feminine values" (love, trust, support, earth, nature, feeling for fellow species, etc..)

- Both assume that these values are best attained in small, personal, cooperative units.

- Both feel that the mega-state (with its mega-corporations, mega-military, and mega-technology) is dead, but that it is better to create new structures rather than to waste time attacking the old.

- Neither withdraws from the world of familiar event, but seeks to ameliorate the present system as it can, at the same time building local cells of rehabilitation within the larger social scene.

- Each recognizes that we are at a crisis moment of history, that abrupt change is inevitable, and that extraordinary efforts will be required to carry us over to the new time.

- Each realizes that women (having discovered certain capacities for change within themselves) will be key agents in aiding men to recognize and reclaim their own human capabilities.

- Therefore, Women's Studies will play an important role as *one* of the sources of the new culture.

- The process of transformation will continue to operate simultaneously in specifically women's areas and in those embracing the full range of human concerns.

Nothing will be lost—everything will be picked up and carried forward into the new era.

"Toto, we are no longer in Kansas."

I went to Lindisfarne. It was my first such conference, my first encounter with the culture of the "new consciousness." I drove and drove, always due West, until I finally arrived at Crestone, Colorado, in the southwest part of the state. There, on a high plateau ringed by mountains, I immediately discovered an artificial lake. Nearby was the resort hotel where the participants were to be housed, and the various buildings associated with it: a meeting house, an airport facility, a golf house, and so on. Down the road was an old ranch house where Thompson and his family were living, as well as his summer students in the subject of sacred architecture. Lindisfarne was building an interdenominational spiritual center higher up the mountain. Other spiritual groups were also planning to locate in the immediate area, building on land donated by a benefactor.

This was, I felt certain, the place I had dreamed of so vividly a few weeks before. It was a "place in the mountains," far to the west of my home. It had a central structure and several buildings nearby, which were loosely connected, but did not comprise a village or a single community. What was most important, it had the artificial lake, which I saw immediately as I looked to the north after I parked my car. I had a deep sense of "coming home."

*Thompson himself was an energetic, highly efficient confer-
ence director. But although he was courteous to everyone, he did
not invite personal confidences. In some ways, he resembled a traditional professor, one more comfortable with a hierarchical
arrangement of teacher-student than with the give and take of
mutual dialogue. The various presenters "spoke to" the audience,
who played the role of onlookers, not participants. Some of the participants were disturbed at this "two-tiered" format, but I was not
troubled, so grateful was I to be included in such august company.*

*The presenters were folk with very unconventional ideas. I
had often encountered radical notions in books, but this was my
first meeting with such advanced thinkers "in the flesh." The
channel David Spangler was there, and Brother David Steindl-
Rast, and Mother Tessa Bielecki (whose daily practice was meditation on the Crucifixion). Also present were the Hulls, founders of
Chinook, a New Age community in the Pacific Northwest; and
James Parks Morton, then dean of the Church of Saint John the
Divine in New York, a church with long-standing ties to
Lindisfarne. They were an impressive group, my first encounter
with others involved in the "New Consciousness."*

*But it was with the other participants—the listeners—that I felt
the closest personal affinity. They were, for the most part, professional people, all successful in their fields, but not (as far as I knew)
world famous. They included college professors, librarians, Jungian
analysts. Some had no particular profession, just a long-term interest in Lindisfarne and the ideas it represented. I felt an incredible
love for and identification with this group. I felt that I could have
easily traded places with any one of them (that is, that we were
reflections of one another, and I might as easily have been them as
myself). This was my first experience of what is sometimes called the
"I am you" phenomenon. I felt that at last, I had found my own "psychic collective." At the same time, I had a deep presentiment that this
particular group would never again come together in this way, and
that I would probably never again visit Lindisfarne.*

*Each evening, we ate a communal meal at the ranch house,
often food that Thompson himself had prepared. He is an excel-*

lent cook. Then, after dinner, we danced in a circle, following the sacred steps of very ancient rituals, to music that had been recorded at Findhorn. For me, this was entry into sacred space.

Since my kundalini experience was so recent (I was still very high, very full of rapturous feeling almost all the time), I urgently wished to discuss it with someone established in the culture of the new age. Since I was not comfortable with the idea of approaching Thompson, who had given me so much through his writing, I spoke with his assistant, a delightful woman who had, like several of the others present, spent time at Findhorn. She was a sympathetic and attentive listener, and I was deeply grateful for her willingness to hear my story. I was surprised that she had not herself experienced kundalini awakening, for I had more or less assumed that everyone at Lindisfarne had undergone this transformative rite.

She had, however, experienced the inner energies in other ways, and recommended that I try massage. I had never had a massage, and didn't understand its connection to the energies, but I vowed to try it as an experiment as soon as an opportunity arose. Such an opportunity did present itself a few weeks later, and the experience was one of deep, sensuous rapture. Since then, I have repeated the experience several times, and can only wonder if others feel the same exquisite bliss, often in such unlikely places as the temples, or the arches of the foot.

When the conference closed, the attendees were invited to respond in a summary session. Here are some notes from which I described my impressions of the week.

The theme for this conference might well be "Amazing Grace." It has been a week filled with "shocking insights."

I came thinking not to be interested. The topic ("Religion and the Future") would not have been my preferred choice. However, I have gained many new insights. One of the most important is the possibility of a "Christian yoga," with the suggestion that these two seemingly disparate ways of opening to God can now be seen as reflections of a single way of allowing God to manifest. It was noted that in some traditions, it is as if God, having given us bodies, prefers that we not acknowledge them. "Christian yoga" suggests an exciting possibility for the reconciliation of spirit and matter.

Another revelation was that of the centrality of the image of Christ on the cross for the contemporary spiritual seeker. Mother Tessa reminded us that for those of us who began in the Christian tradition, this image is permanently fixed in our psyches. All of us carry a "sleeping Christ" within, and we need to come to terms with its meaning, to unfold the image into a new vision, for the mystery of resurrection does not exclude the mystery of pain and compassion.

Each evening, we performed sacred dancing.

One morning a tai chi dancer performed alone by the lake. He seemed to glitter as he moved. Together, these became my image of the conference: The group coming together as a whole in the communion of the dance, while to one side the solitary dancer enacts his own oneness with the surroundings.

Perhaps it is better to say that sometimes there comes an image of the single dancer—a one—and sometimes the image expands to become the group—a many—for of course they are the same.

The Doctrine of the Other

Emerson called it "Oversoul," Yeats the "Daemon," Hindus the "Brahma/Atman," and Buddhists "Buddha Nature." Kabbalists speak of "Adam Kadmon," modern Christians of the "Christ-nature." Whatever its "name," it is the sense of the other, the elevated, the self raised to the highest power. For it is the essential self, the resident being, lifted, amplified, perfected. And this, the higher nature, strives ceaselessly to live through, express by way of, and ultimately unite with the lower part.

A Near Abortion

As a child, I felt much alienation, inner soul sickness, and depression. My parents provided much love and care; indeed, in many ways I was pampered. I suffered none of the traumas so many now reveal from their early years, of family violence or extreme abuse of one kind or another. But, although in many ways I was lucky to be born to good, kind, healthy parents, something "inside" seemed to lament perpetually. I felt as though, somehow, I had been thrust into an unsought alliance, that I was someone else's unwelcome burden.

Recently, a month ago, my mother revealed that I was a near abortion. *(Abortion among married women was surprisingly common at this time.)* She had already scheduled the physician's appointment, stood ready to take the prescribed medication the night before, when "something stayed her hand." Mind you, she had already had two abortions previously (and would have another in the years to follow). She meant business. It was the late 1920s, and times were hard in this part of the country. Large families were a water slide to poverty. (How my parents dreaded that word. They grew up when it was loaded with meaning: worn-out shoes; ill-fitting dresses; monotonous winter diets; families who got starved out, burned out, bugged out. It was a reality then, not a literary or poetical theme.)

"I don't know why," my mother said, confessing to me at last after more than fifty years. "I just couldn't do it. Something said not to do it."

I joined the ranks of those who were gratuitously spared, who stood in line but stepped aside at the last moment and did not purchase the ticket for the plane that crashed, who walked *around* the ladder from which the workman dropped a chunk of wood or stone, who refused the suspect potato salad at the picnic—all those who were plucked out, miraculously passed over, by God, or fate, or chance, whatever it is that controls our lives.

I tell myself, it is a miracle any of us get here at all. Mathematically, it is not possible that any of us were ever conceived or born. The odds are too overwhelmingly against it. Yet here we are.

I am a Westerner. My family were Irish (and Welsh and English, a few) emigrants. Early in the nineteenth century, they came to the New World seeking land. My own roots are close to the frontier. Everything in my heritage suggests the "outward":

doing, acting, fighting to survive. My ancestors struggled to wrest food and cotton from bare soil. Later, my father sold things—automobiles, newspapers, houses. Life was a constant effort to win, convince others. But I was a dreamy child. I spent hours staring into the grilles of the gas fire. I kept my nose in a book, wouldn't come when called. I found that "inside" was better than "outside." I did not fit the Western pattern of the active one, the doer.

What does it mean when kundalini *happens* to a Westerner? The verb here is important. The experience *occurs to* the passive object, the subject thus emerging as a nonbeing, a not-self, an "other." No amount of activity can *make* kundalini happen. Further, it occurs typically when one is "emptied out," "vacated," having surrendered ego, the core of self. And this death is not without its pain.

Bliss in the Head

Today, I again felt much bliss in the head during meditation and yoga. This is sweet, soothing, like a cool breeze blowing over the temples. The bliss was unplanned, unexpected—did missing a meal last night contribute?

I have been reading Gopi Krishna's book on the spontaneous arousal of kundalini in his body. His experience was nothing like mine. He experienced much pain and agony. The energy released was too intense. It nearly overwhelmed his system. Once the jet was opened, it could not be turned off. My experience seems to be patterned after Christian mystical paths.

A Delicate, Sweet-Limbed Krishna

Again, I experienced bliss in the head during meditation and yoga. It is almost like grace. I am very grateful. The only image required is that of a delicate, sweet-limbed Krishna, sitting with legs easily resting in a lotus position.

There is something within me that deeply and overwhelmingly resists detailing this most central of experiences, describing that which has been most significant in turning my life. As long as it remains essentially undefined, a loose shape floating in the near distance, one can think of it in comfortable terms—a specter to be called close, brought into focus for intentional scrutiny at any time. Vague outlines, wavering forms—these tranquilize and soothe through their dreamlike nature. In one direction, the image slips toward an impulse. To move it into thought—precise, determined, exact, contingent—is another matter.

Some Questions on Kundalini

What is kundalini? From where does its energy arise? Snake, flower, bird—each in a way metaphorically describes some aspect of its manifestation. But does it have a physiological base or pattern, a traceable path of action?

Why does it manifest as sexual energy in the head? Why is it sexually pleasurable? What is the physical source of any pleasant sexual feeling? Is it merely the flow of blood through certain vessels located in the genital area? Does increase of pressure beget pleasure? If so, why here and not in other bodily regions like toes, wrists, or navel? If increase of blood flowing through the head produces bliss, why don't we get "turned on" by standing on our heads?

Why is this phenomenon so rare, if it is part of a normal human repertoire? If it follows a basic pattern (ego death, pleasure, oneness with the external world), what is the connection between these various stages? What are chakras? What are the connections between sexual thought and sexual feeling (e.g., brain and body)? Why is there so much diversity in the theories of kundalini—as to number, nature, activity of chakras (whether to "feel" a chakra is good or bad, whether chakras turn like wheels or bloom like flowers)?

These questions reveal my state of innocence at this early stage. I was a naïf, one lacking instruction or instructor. Subsequently, I discovered some answers, but I found that much mystery still surrounds the kundalini process. I learned much from my own experience: for example, I realized that the bliss waves can indeed awaken "toes, wrists, or navel," in fact, any and all parts of the system. Dr. Lawrence Edwards, a recognized authority and teacher on the kundalini process, offers (in personal correspondence) the following explanation of the subtle body:

> The subtle body, the sushumna nadi (the central channel), the chakras, the coiled form of the Shakti, the power of Consciousness manifesting these subtle yet enormously potent energy patterns are all superphysical. The intersecting nadis that form the chakras are mysterious energy channels, like beams of light whose forms are maintained without a physical container, are hubs where these energy channels cross and move out to expand and create our personal universe.

I later learned that the primary chakras, or subtle energy centers, are located along the spine from the root (base of the spine) to the crown (top of the skull). Others exist at the level of the sexual organs, the solar plexus, the heart, the throat, and the forehead (sometimes called the third eye). The word chakra is translated as "wheel," for the ancient yogis thought of the centers as wheels which turned as the energies passed through. Some systems such as Tibetan Buddhist recognize only five major centers.

The larger question of why the flowing superphysical energies may produce bodily bliss awaits further explanation, as does the whole area of somatic response to specific stimuli.

A Zen Master

In early August, Kate and I traveled to Boulder, where I was to attend an international meditation conference sponsored by one of the Tibetan centers there. During the week of the conference, His Holiness the Dalai Lama arrived in Boulder to speak. Kate and I arrived early to be sure we got a good seat in the coliseum.

When the Dalai Lama appeared, these followers arose and bowed before him, paying homage to his exalted position. I felt uncomfortable with this, as if the devotees were insisting on his status as a god; by their actions, they seemed to divide the group into "insiders" and "outsiders." When the Dalai Lama spoke, I recognized a gentle, kindly man of great personal dignity and honor. But I had no sense of being in the presence of a deity. His words were true, but they were in essence the beliefs of anyone who loves peace and wishes to see a world in universal harmony. On the whole, I was more disappointed than inspired. As in my dream, I, in effect, "could not find a seat" in this particular assembly.

More important to me was my encounter with Eido Roshi, Zen master from New York City, who was one of the presenters at the conference, which was called "Meditation East and West."

"As you are now, I once was," I thought as I observed him, for he evoked great nostalgia on my part. I indeed recognized him as one such as I had been, in some other time or place. He was brother to my "monk in the window." He was smiling, balanced, at ease—truly a delightful man, making sly jokes, playing. A rounded man of medium height, he wore his Zen priest robes (I had never seen these before, and was quite impressed.) He seemed at home with the group and in the world.

As he came into the hall, I sent him a desperate mental message. I needed help—needed a method of meditation which was quieter, less challenging than kundalini as I was then practicing it. I needed to find a gentler path into the self. I demanded (mentally) his assistance. (I did not at the time know that such demands can, in fact, be directed at a Zen master, and that he is obligated to respond. I acted from instinct or intuition, or perhaps some part of me did know.)

Next day, at the beginning of the group Zen meditation (about two hundred were in attendance), his tall, vital spiritual assistant seemed to seek me out; he took a cushion next to me, but was immediately called away to other duties. I felt that he had come over to discover what it was I needed.

After the meditation, Eido Roshi spoke. As he concluded, he looked at me, and I at him, for one brief instant. Again, I demanded help of him, and for a moment his eyes flashed wide in what seemed a startled recognition.

I never saw him again.

However, I soon began to ease into a "gentler meditation," primarily through shifting my attention from the image of Shiva/Shakti, to that of Krishna.

Each day now, I experience much bliss in the head during meditation; these sweet vibrations continue during most of the day. I meditate once or twice daily. Sometimes there is bliss in the head and body (first and second chakras) as well. Often, it flows in the head alone. I grow stable, secure. And colors are very pure, as they were during the initiation of last May, and as they were when I was eighteen, and "unfallen."

Purity is the theme. And that includes the body (recognizing its inherent purity).

Did the Zen master answer my plea? Did a subconscious element of his spirit make contact with a "higher self" of mine? Did I simply use this experience as a metaphor or impetus to discover for myself a solution I needed? No matter, I have found that which I sought. Full kundalini is indeed much more powerful; it might lead me more quickly to greater energy, enabling me to produce larger changes in my environment. But this other way feels much more comfortable; it is what I can deal with, the level of that which is me.

"Now I am the same, but different."

Illness, Accident, Aches and Pains

In late August, I resumed teaching. Shortly thereafter, my mother became seriously ill. The multiple stresses began to tell on me. I began to experience strange aches and pains in various parts of my body. By October, I was an easy "convert" when a teacher of Transcendental Meditation solicited me for instruction into the specific technique followed by this group. She asserted that I needed someone experienced in meditation to guide me, and implied that by following the TM method, virtually all my problems would disappear. I was "initiated" into TM in a lovely ceremony, but found that, although the world did indeed take on a beautiful radiance thereafter, my physical complaints seemed to intensify rather than to diminish. I began to develop severe headaches, backaches, and stomachaches—my entire biological system seemed to go into revolt. But I had pledged to give TM a fair trial, and kept at it, doggedly, for the next five or six months. Finally, after my headaches had become so painful that I was scheduled for a brain scan to check for possible tumor, I concluded that TM was not the right method for me.

I had continued writing in my journal throughout this difficult period, but it was not easy to describe any of these events—whether of bliss or pain—with any accuracy. I felt I needed more distance.

There was, of course, no tumor, or any ulcer, or other physical problem. A process that had freely manifested in its original expression had been thwarted and blocked because of the pressures of work, family issues, and the attempt—via TM—to channel energies into unfamiliar paths. TM "replaced" my familiar gods and goddesses (of whom there had been many, all dynamic sources of energy), with a mantra that was to me highly disturbing. Thus, in effect, by changing from one system of meditation to another, I capped or stifled that vibrant flow that had risen so splendidly in the early days of my experience. TM paid no heed to feeling levels. It was all mental. Once again, my head was severed from my body. I learned here a drastic lesson in the dangers of abandoning the instruction of the "inner guru" to embrace an external teacher.

For so long now, my life has been captive to external events. The illness and suffering of my mother and father, the serious (potentially fatal) automobile accident of Kate (on a Saturday in September about two weeks ago). I have no time for inner contemplation, introspection giving way to outer concern for these, the sufferers of this world.

My mother—my call to her found her hospitalized, so weak she could not sit alone or feed herself. My father is worn to exhaustion (he is now eighty-seven), weeping hysterically at every moment of what he assumed was the final crisis. Then a stay in a "rest home," the only one available on short notice, where she got no rest at all. Where people screamed and howled and moaned day and night, like idiots raving against the injustice of a malevolent fate. Abandoned all, some strove to continue a form of life, albeit grossly reduced. They crept along the corridors on canes and crutches and metal sticks. Some bent double over their aluminum walkers. Some lurched forward in mechanical chairs. Some propelled themselves, inch by inch, with their own hands.

Edna Pinkerton (my mother's roommate) explained each day that she was ninety-four years old, that she tried not to be any trouble, that she lived in a nearby town, but had no one to stay with her. On returning from dinner each evening, she rang for a bedpan. Sometimes the aide arrived in time, sometimes not. The aides preferred to let her sit—solitary and in pain—in her wheelchair until the other residents were attended to and it was convenient to take care of Edna. Once I got them to transfer her to bed early, but now that I no longer go there, I judge she is left sitting, propped up by her pain, hour after hour, until someone remembers or takes pity on her.

Yet these bent ones, these stooped, drained, misshapen beings, presented a claim upon the heart one could not deny. What response was possible but total pity? What reaction could one feel but awed compassion in the presence of absolute being, past (lifted, transcended, passed out of) all concern for appearance or station or name, or (for many) family connection or past life or even memory of yesterday's pain. Here was humanity reduced to its basic, absolute dimension—that which is, which seeks neither to justify or explain; to the common state, the ultimate purgation before the last transition.

In the midst of this panorama of grief lay my mother repeating, "This is nearest to Hell I ever expect to come." And I sat by her side for five days, and thought of our life together, and her life before and after me, and set all other thoughts aside.

Finally, we got her home. With a hearty nurse who could have been Juliet's attendant in Shakespeare's play of the doomed lovers. My mother grew stronger each day, until she could feed herself, and sit up with aid, and drag her feeble feet slowly forward with support on either side.

Then Kate, driving east on a city street, was hit broadside by a car traveling south. *(Kate's "affair" had long since terminated. We were still together, but on somewhat uneasy terms. I was no longer capable of total trust.)* The tiny VW Bug was smashed by the giant Cadillac—coming at full speed across the intersection. I was not there, but with my mother. I learned the details the next day on my return.

Kate had no broken bones, few external bruises or cuts. The car was wrecked totally. The side was crushed, the windshield cracked (by Kate's skull). The steering column bent (by Kate's chest). The side and rear windows were blown out. It was as close to death as any of us would ever wish to come.

Kate had been on her way to buy flowers for M.'s grave when the accident happened. (M. was her high school teacher she loved so much—M. had saved her life once before, when Kate "overdosed" in high school.) Kate thinks that M.'s spirit "threw a protective shield" around her at the time of the accident. Such would seem to be the case—Kate came through relatively unscathed (the driver of the larger car was not hurt, either). McGuire, the sheepdog, was thrown out the back windshield; she spun around on the pavement, then jumped and ran from the scene in a panic. She was found, finally, several miles away, after she had dropped in exhaustion. Her only apparent damage was sore feet (her pads were almost worn away).

What with my concern for the suffering of those closest to me, with my trips to visit my mother every weekend (she lives some 150 miles away), my terror and grief for Kate's near catastrophe, the series of interviews at school for two weeks (we are selecting a candidate to fill a position in the program), I have been far too busy to think, much less write, about events for weeks. The tranquil meditation has continued. I still feel it is the proper choice for me. I had reached a point in my earlier practice where I seemed to fall into a meditative state instantly, and even to maintain this state during much of the day as I went about my activities. It was then I decided to take instruction in Transcendental Meditation. My prospective "teacher" suggested I drop my usual meditation until I learned this new method. I have meditated irregularly since then.

Why do I take lessons in something I can already do? Because I want contact with others involved in a technique. Because I am open to possibility. To help the teacher out. To have a new experience. To see how much further I can progress.

My "teacher" and her friend do "flying." This intrigues, because it is an exercise in levitation that is described in ancient literature (initiates of yoga are said to "hop like frogs"). Supposedly, it is evidence of spiritual advancement. Obviously, Maharshi, the guru who introduced this form of meditation to the West, is in touch with something.

I did not go to see my mother this weekend. I went to town to catch the 7:20 A.M. bus Saturday morning, but forgot my purse. My subconscious discovered a way for me to stay home for a much-needed vacation.

Did I mention the dream of the chair? Before my mother became ill, I dreamed I went to visit a student of mine. She had an adult "potty-chair" in her living room. I had to use it while visiting her. I thought it rather vulgar—it reminded me of an old fashioned "birthing chair." On my next visit home, I found such a chair by my mother's bed in her bedroom (she was by then in the hospital). Now she is at home; she lies in the "den" with her chair next to her. So the dream was prophetic.

I had no sense that Kate had been in an accident at the time it occurred. Yet I have long been apprehensive about this particular car, since when we first test drove it, I distinctly smelled blood and had a strong fear that Kate would be killed in that car. The premonition was too close for comfort, as it turns out. Why did I let her purchase it without protest? Because such omens seem silly when they threaten to rule our lives. Because the car seemed a good buy in terms of condition, appearance, and so on. Because it had a peculiar odor of gasoline, which may have been (literally) what I smelled.

So because of events happening externally, I have had little chance to be in touch (consciously) internally. My TM teacher spoke of people undergoing "purification by suffering" before they begin to meditate. Indeed, purification seems a correct term for such experience. At times I felt flattened out to a single dimension, with nothing of me, the self, remaining. Tomorrow is the "introductory lecture"; the other lessons come soon thereafter.

A Picture that Vibrates

I was initiated into Transcendental Meditation. The ceremony was more than I expected. We took off our shoes, went into a bedroom containing an altar on which were a picture of Guru Dev (Maharishi's guru) and the gifts I had brought (flowers, fruit, and a white handkerchief). Then came my teacher singing and speaking Sanskrit. There was a definite sense of the guru's presence. I was acutely aware of the sternness of his face. My teacher and I both knelt, then rose, and she "gave" (spoke) my mantra; I did not even realize what she had done. I was left alone to meditate, and I "became" in imagination a familiar but not fully identified figure—the young Eastern prince, perhaps. This image has been with me often before.

The picture of Guru Dev wavered and vibrated, as human faces often do when I am staring at them to discover the "face behind the face" (perhaps a previous incarnation). I've never seen a picture do this before. In fact, I have noted that images on the TV screen, for example, have no aura, nor do they vibrate. But, though the face vibrated as with intense inner energy, it was unsmiling, almost forbidding.

As for the mantra, it seemed absolutely foreign and strange. For the first several meditations thereafter, I fought it—I wanted to give it back. It seemed to strangle or to cut me, like a buzz saw. But the teacher reassured me and from then on it seemed okay. Yet I wondered why what before had seemed so natural (meditating on images) seemed so forced with this new technique.

On Saturday, I traveled four hours by bus to see my mother. The trip was a mystical journey as color, cloud, tree conspired to create "nirvana in samsara," Heaven on Earth. The day was fogbound, mysterious. How is it possible to bear such intense beauty?

My mother was infinitely improved. The visit was, however, filled with old tensions rediscovered, of parent and child, of age and its impatient critic (me), of the difficulties of expressing love. My return trip was one in which I rode through glorious autumn beauty, but I never connected with it. It never penetrated me.

On Sunday we (TM students and teachers) had a group meditation as a foursome. I felt myself grow or swell out (like a bubble) until I touched the "bubbles" of the others. Then yet another bubble formed overhead to connect us all. It was an unusual experience. On Monday, I had more elation and more sense of beauty, and some giggles. On Tuesday, I simply felt "normal," as though everything had, finally, fallen into place. I saw the beauty about me and accepted it without deep emotional involvement. I said to myself, "Now I need nothing more—I have everything I could wish." I asked my teacher how to bear the sense of wonderment, the deeply flushed colors of the world. "You'll get used to it," she answered.

Within minutes of writing the above, I felt ill—with upset stomach, aches and pains of various kinds. I thought I had the flu, a virus, what have you. I located the trouble, finally. I realized how upset I was over the upcoming case of my colleague/friend (the one I had had the disagreement with earlier), who was now preparing to sue the university for salary redress. Now I feel a deep loyalty to the dean, who has given me such support through the years. Yet I fear that by remaining loyal to him I will provoke her anger and I could grow ill as a consequence. Hers was the face I saw in my own when I looked in the mirror during the awakening experience of last May. I carry a special responsibility for her, a karmic bond perhaps. But how can I honor this obligation without betraying my dean?

Today I feel almost well. I stayed home (I had no classes scheduled to teach) and read my notebooks of recent months. The world looks clear, sharp, purified, good. Again, I tried to connect this response with some specific period in my past, but without success.

Colors Washed Clear

In meditation this morning, I for the first time saw a circle of light (but not very bright). I focused on the center with joy and felt good after the meditation. I felt that I had truly "gone in," lost consciousness of surroundings, but I was still aware of my breath.

Today, again, there is a deep sense of purity, of colors washed clear to the basic essence. And because of this—the revised hues, restored tinctures—I have again the sense of return to some early stage of youth or childhood. I feel I am reliving a state or mood, perhaps of a particular day years ago when the colors looked like this. But I cannot recall any particular event, or time, or age, connected with this present look of the world. Yet it is familiar, and of this life. Long ago it washed through me, and now, it repeats. Possibly to bring happiness where grief rode before. I think that saints must see the world this way (though I am no saint, by any definition).

In the vocabulary of alchemical transmutation, this is a stage of purifying. We purify, and condense (congeal), purify and coagulate, and thus we fix our matter into gold.

In other terms, when the gods are ready to act, they shake you and shake you and shake again. The threatening male student, Kate's unexpected involvement, kundalini, Lindisfarne, the Zen Roshi at Boulder and his gift of quiet meditation, my parents' illness with the various traumas it involved. Again and again we are shaken, tossed, until at last we surrender all—will, desire, inclination—our only wish to conform to that which flows in and through us, to become *that which we are,* not through an act of will but by a state of quiet acceptance. We give in to the current, letting it carry us to an unknown destination, trusting to its direction and energy to deliver us to the next tumultuous passage.

Although I cannot connect this sense of purity to a specific past moment, it does recall to me the way I felt at Eleusis, Greece, in the spring of 1977; the first weeks (years, even) of living in Boulder in the 1960s; my encounter with Christian Science in my teens; even the autumn of 1969, a time of love in the mountains.

Finding Silence

It is as if, after pursuing *words* for so many decades, I emerge in the wordless realm. Mind, body, senses—nothing leads to a final truth. Only in silence can the word be spoken; only in darkness can the light shine forth.

Seeing Auras

After I began TM, not only nature but *people* appeared more and more beautiful. On Wednesday, when I walked into my class, I saw *everyone* in their highest beauty. I wondered if I could bear it.

Also, I have begun to see more auras. The other evening, I saw pale yellow around two friends, but one also had a mantle of dark purple (almost black) over her face and throat. At school at a round table meeting, I saw pale rainbows circling the heads of several speakers, and a golden cone entering the head of one (my TM teacher). And later I saw one pinkish-gold aura, high and extremely spiked, above a friend who was very upset at the time.

I am getting a sense of "going in deeper" during meditation and a sense of "balancing out" during daily experience. But when I say my mantra, I often experience disturbing vibrations in my head.

Meeting with Silence

Why should I fall into you,
backwards spiral into nothingness,
empty of words, images gone
as if dissolved in an acrid bowl?

You say, so that I may meet with Brahma,
face turned to facelessness,
confronting "bliss of the real,"
sans quality, without sound.
I say, for centuries I labored
to mass this body, shape this breast.
What flows through me a current
of my own devising,
even now the molecules ping their secrets,
blood-tones shimmering
their shameless joy.

Eastern Religion and Western Thought

Eastern religion and the new physics (as well as certain aspects of Western psychology) have much in common. They both assert:

- The nonreality of the "self."

- The nonreality of the physical universe.

- The nonreality of seeming interaction between self and the external universe.

- The theory of transformations (for one, through reincarnation; for the other [physics] through physical transmutation, as of solids into gas, or matter into energy).

- The vibrational undercurrent of *all* "reality."

- A nonverbal (unconscious or pre-conscious) level of awareness, as well as a verbal level.

- The oneness of all systems.

- A "relational" reality as the only reality (what a thing is in relation to others is the only thing it is—it is *defined* by relationship).

Once more, I asked questions of my inner teacher:

Q. Why did the West (historically) take a predominantly masculine (divisive, rational, linear, logical, materialistic) path to
"reality"? Why did the East take a holistic, feminine, intuitive,
nonrational, body approach?

A. Because the East was more attuned to the body. Judaism, in
certain respects, denounced the body as evil. Greek philosophy
rejected the body as inferior. The yogis devised a system based
upon and revealed through the body. Thus, body and mind
were not separate, but were held to be *one* in the union of yoga.

The West failed to explore and develop this path. They failed
to discover the sacred uses of the body. Being acquainted only
with its "profane" employments (for sexuality, procreation),
they relegated it to the realm of the abhorrent, and labeled it
the source of all evil.

The body had long been esteemed and reverenced in the
mother religions. Worship of the Mother Goddess was central
to Eastern yogic cults. The body became an instrument to
achieve union—not only through the loins but in the head as
well. The West, knowing little or nothing of such transgenital
coupling, denounced the flesh as sinful, corrupt in and of
itself, since it led not toward but away from the Creator.

For the East, God is immanent in the corporal self, and this
(God) is but another (higher) reflection of one's own essence.
For the Westerner, the body may be permitted to function for
divine purposes, but only under certain carefully prescribed
conditions, in rituals enacted according to highly specific laws

(for example, sexual intercourse between properly married heterosexual pairs). All other manifestation of divine energy within the body (in a specifically "sexual" or even pleasurable sense) is renounced as suspect, part of the devil's show.

So, ultimately, the tragic flaw of Western rationality was its insistence on dichotomy: mind/body, male/female, good/evil. Hatred of the female led to a deadly bifurcation of reality, and a subsequent history of one-sided vision. To retrace its steps and recoup its loss, the West will have to accept and reaffirm the feminine principle as coexistent with the male in every being, man or woman.

Q. What about a method such as Transcendental Meditation in which the body is lost from consciousness, the mind is emptied, and thought itself is vacated? Is this the tranquillity that reigns beyond the ecstatic union? Is it the silence which underlies *all* speech? Is it the qualityless reality that is antecedent to the world of particularized forms?

A. In kundalini, we envision our interior "female" divine in union with our interior "male" divine: the energy thus produced rises, leading us to ecstatic union with the radiant essence of life itself. It flashes into the brain and again travels down the spine. Upward and downward together lead us into bliss; we are aware of a state of being, not of the overall nature of our being. Asked "Who are you?" at this peak moment, we can only answer, "I am one who feels bliss." Later, restored to ordinary consciousness, our reply to the same query must be: "I am the one who *experienced* the bliss and if I am fortunate may do so again."

This moment, then, becomes the pivot point of our reality, the container of that which is most essentially and undeniably ourselves. The rest is insubstantial stuff, the play of Maya which can seduce us no more.

Kundalini is the path of ecstasy, TM the path of tranquillity. One carries sensation to its highest pitch in order to obtain power (energy). The other dissolves sensation (as well as image) in order to attain a state of harmony. Kundalini ultimately leads outward, to projects, ideas, achievement; TM moves the spirit into its own interior, from which it quietly observes in its most beautiful and positive form the action of the world, with little desire to intervene or participate. Does one wish to be actor or observer? Agent or spectator?

Such dichotomy is, of course, only partly true. The transcendental meditator seeks to introduce a "new vibration" into the human sphere, thus ameliorating the vast turmoil of the agitated world.

A Hindu Yogi

When I look back over the notes for this year, I realize I have said nothing about the "Hindu yogi" who seemed to come forward (as if we two shared one body) during the experiences of last spring. During the early days of my "initiation," when I was first discovering the energies, yantra meditation, yoga, and other things, it seemed as if this "inner being" (or alternate, buried aspect of self) emerged, and for a while he dominated (or at least directed) my life. I thought of him as Hindu, for he was extremely fastidious, insisting on frequent showers and absolute cleanliness of person. He was highly selective in what he wore, what he ate, and where he slept (he preferred a hard mat on the floor to the bed I was used to).

When I did yoga for the first time, and so easily fell into the rapture of union, I decided that I must have been a yogi in some previous lifetime. Hence I thought of my emergent inner self as a "Hindu yogi." (Although, of course, my imagery and method of visualization were primarily Tibetan Buddhist, I think, however, that all these streams [Hindu, Buddhist, Tantric] crossed and ran together in many ways in earlier times.)

A Year of Prophecy and Fulfillment

This is the time of year when magic proceeds from the light. Something, perhaps, about the Earth's angle to the Sun in winter—an axis tilts and everything fills with beauty. Such sharpness and clarity. In particular, I remember the journey to see the whales in California in late December years ago. Also, the look of the Earth, of trees and rusted walls, before our trip to Europe in 1976 (and the look of things there also). It is as if a layer has been peeled away, a veneer stripped, to reveal an essential, naked, absolute purity.

This has been a year of prophecy and fulfillment. Last year's pages foretell this year as a time of change, as indeed it was. Central to the whole was initiation in late May: "graduation time." That initiation was preceded by loss—like a test in which one relinquishes one's most valuable possession in order to gain what is even more valuable. Having given all, one receives all. And even that which is lost is restored.

Prophetic themes were many as were the dreams: of one who leaves and yet remains; arriving at places long sought as an ultimate, paradisiacal destination, a hospital chair. There were many internal images, including the symbol LO! and its many transfigurations, all reflecting the fusion of the human and divine; there is the poem of the dramatic coming of the Mother, which foretold a future experience. There was, over a year ago, the repetition of a pattern—the activation of the male principle for Kate and me.

Then a rejection of the more intense modes of experiencing higher energies (kundalini). The seeking of quieter, gentler means of access through TM. A teacher was sought, and a teacher came, to heal the hectic excitement of the summer, which was compounded by the parental traumas of the fall. And now the world looks beautiful, and sometimes I see auras, as I have always wished. Kate sometimes joins me in meditation (she, too, took instruction in TM).

TM did more—and less—than I had expected. It brought the sense of joy, pure color, occasional glimpses of the inner soul/beauty of others. It helped develop the nascent capacity for seeing auras. It left me better prepared to cope with the world. However, as yet, I lack the energy, drive, and intensity of the kundalini experience. Kundalini rushes forth at once: one is "reborn" in an instant, accumulating sufficient power in minutes for months of activity and creation. TM builds more slowly and, I hope, more solidly.

Further, the actual meditation periods of TM seem not to provide as much pleasure—no union of the gods in the head. Meditating alone, I find my head squeezing or faintly aching; strange flutters and vibrations traverse my scalp and even plunge to the inner brain. Meditating with others, I feel surging energy in the head, almost as if I have connected to a power source slightly too strong for me.

But I have had two definite strikes against me with TM: I entered at a state of great personal tension, anguish, even; and menopause has announced itself unequivocally (as pain and stiffness in the back, legs, and head).

Another source of disappointment is that I have felt deeply the loss of my symbols, the gods and goddesses who visited in imagination, the picturing by which certain truths—present or future—were revealed. Sometimes I have felt that the "vacuity" of the nonimagistic state reflects God's own primal condition, when to alleviate His loneliness he created the myriad beings of the world.

For a while, I feared to lose my visual imagination entirely. Perhaps because I had engaged in an alternative technique, I was more fully aware of something missing. Now, however, I grow less and less cognizant of any lack. What is offered is an energy flow, almost too intense for adequate response.

Kundalini Energy Is Intense

Kundalini energy is sensuous in tone, and it expresses itself, initially, as arousal in the lower centers. It is deep, intense, cutting, like a snake biting through the muscle and membrane. Then it "rises," lifting the feelings upward toward the navel. About this time, one becomes aware of a physical delight in the head, almost erotic. Sweet energies flow upward and downward. The lower body is connected to the brain by a stream of delight, simultaneously flowing away from and toward the poles of activity, the entire process sustained by incredible ecstatic energies streaming into the crown from above.

This is the ancients' "intercourse of the gods" within the head. It is the primordial union of human and divine. It leads to awe, as the human, passive recipient, is filled with the essential energy of creation, which is vast, incomprehensible, indifferent to all but its own expression. It is as little personalized as any natural experience and confirms, as always, that the natural at the level of vital source is the divine.

How do we do this? For years, we visualize gods and goddesses in all their sensuous attraction, arriving to participate, to fuse with ourselves, in the act of love. We experience the divine male, the divine female, as self, or partner, or absorb both as ultimate principle into our psyche. We then experience a loss—a sudden deprivation of something or someone so integral to our own identity that we have long since ceased to view it as separate from ourselves. In absence, in lack, a vacuum exists. The "ego" (sense of self) is dissolved. We suffer a deep death, extreme in its pain and agony, both physical and mental. We feel that we are nothing within. Then, gradually, we become aware that our independent existence can continue even after such devastating loss and that certain compensations may follow. We begin to feel better, and then to feel good in body and spirit. We surrender that which is of most value to us, and experience a restoration of self.

Then at the peak of our powers with unresolved energy freely floating through our system, we contemplate an image of the divine couple in union. Because by now we incorporate both male and female, we experience an immediate charge in our lower centers. Suddenly, something happens in the brain. An experience that before was physical becomes mental, located above. The bliss flows simultaneously through lower and higher centers. ("As above, so below.") We recognize it, but feel great wonder as if an elbow or wrist suddenly became a sexual center.

There is a sense of a thousand petals unfolding in the head, each released into its own point of ecstasy, and our body moves toward a point of "mental orgasm," which can never be realized, because it would "short out" the brain. After a few minutes (during which intensity is maintained by *experiencing* rather than *witnessing* the process, by *being* not *observing*), we close, and know that we have, finally and forever, joined body and spirit, human and cosmic divine, form and feeling.

The power-flow tells us this is our source, the streaming dynamic of life itself, above rationality, beyond morality—the Being Who floods the manifested universe (Maya) and makes it move. It is "that which is."

This energy moves the cosmos, flowing into whatever is *open to receive it*. We take into our beings as much as we are prepared to admit. To open to it is to be charged with an intensity that can heighten or else obliterate our potentials. For this reason—its power to annihilate the unprepared—it must be approached with caution. It is like an electric current that can rejuvenate or destroy, as circumstances dictate. Even Moses did not look on the Face of the Lord. Ishmael in Melville's *Moby Dick* was content to see only the backside, the "upflukes," of the godlike whale. Kundalini power is ultimate force. But force can be turned against the self if one is not prepared to control it.

A Delicate Ecstasy

Today after careful preparation (hot shower, yoga, breathing) I meditated and fell into a mild ecstasy. This time I permitted myself to listen to music so that I experienced a blend of ecstatic feeling that arose from *two* sources (the music and the meditation). Also, I permitted myself to visualize a young Asian boy (my double, either now living or my future self).

This is precisely what I sought—a kind of "mild" kundalini, a delicate ecstasy that soothes and enchants, delivering no shocks or traumas. Thus the experience satisfies the earlier expressed need to include the body in the total experience.

William Irwin Thompson speaks of "sexualizing the brain." I agree, but not in the sense that the feeling moves toward desire, but as it points toward joy or bliss, states of celebration in which one participates a "self-validating experience," which seeks no goal other than to fully know (be) itself. One seeks nothing outside the self, for there is completion arising from the "wonderfull."

The Last Vision: Christ on the Cross

The last vision of my awakening was Christ on the Cross. I was much surprised at this, for I assumed that Christian symbolism no longer operated in my psyche. I witnessed the vision, and interpreted it as an exposition of pain. I felt compassion, a lowering of vibrational intensity as I took the suffering into myself. Then I raised the vibrations back and felt I had been instructed as to how to heal others.

I was again much surprised to find (later) that Bhagwan Shree Rajneesh asserts (in *Meditation: The Art of Ecstasy*) that the last vision (before the mind drops) will be a savior figure from the knower's own background:

> The last vision to be seen is of a central religious figure. . . . To a Christian (and by Christian I mean one who has imbibed the language of Christianity, the symbols of Christianity. . . . from his very childhood), the figure of Jesus on the cross will be the last.
>
> The mind cannot conceive of anything abstractly, so the last effort of the mind to understand reality, will be through the symbol that has been most important to it. . . . [T]he opening of the sahasrar is the utmost that is possible with the mind. The last figure . . . the archetype—will come.

Now, I did not go into a full *samadhi.* I stayed in a state of trancelike ecstasy for several days, but always with a sense that I would "return." My expectation was to go back into the world, to function as a personality in that world. I also felt that I had gone my full limit—to have penetrated further into the experience (or to have allowed it to penetrate me further), would have been far too risky.

A Whirling Pool in a Magic Lake

It was the sort of moment toward which everything in life is directed, and later, from which all thereafter flows. It was a key, a watershed, a whirling pool in a magic lake into which all is pulled, to reappear afterward at another place (the other side of reality), but transformed, reconstituted according to a higher principle.

To describe it, one must summon memories of other personal firsts, such as the first movement of a planchette across a surface of letters, responding meaningfully to a casual inquiry. Something that transcends limits, which goes to the border and then crosses a perimeter, which says irrevocably, "No, the realms are not divided; there is another reality impinging on your own of which you are a part and which constantly interpenetrates your existence in every way."

The kundalini experience was unlike any other. To discover energy in the loins was a commonly shared human phenomenon, strange (once one thought about it) but universally reported. To send desire into the head (as physical sensation, not thought)—who has heard of, much less encountered, such a bizarre event? The ancient metaphors rose and took on sudden meaning: pagans having intercourse "with the gods" in age-old ceremonies; Eastern bodhisattvas with lotus petals unfolding in their skulls, bringing bliss. This, then, was ultimate initiation. This was the union of divine energy and human substance. I reveled in feeling and knew that sheer *delight* was the basis, the unifying oneness, of "reality." To deny delight was to deny God, to cut myself off from bliss was to say "no" to the Source.

But the Source is as impersonal as it is vast. It is like a gigantic power supply roaming the universe, or rather encircling and penetrating it, available for ecstatic union with any being, creature, or thing, that would admit it, not turn it away. Our conscious minds are like insistent valves constantly turning off, shutting down, closing the very channels that might admit this vital stream. To be energized is to be infused with feeling. One becomes a pivot, a point of entry, an ecstatic meeting place of mind and matter.

Later on, as I moved deeper into my experience, I revised some of my thought on the impersonal nature of this fundamental energy. I came to know kundalini as an intelligent force of Divine Love. The Beloved Within was not a metaphor but the ultimate expression of union with the Sublime Reality. As one observer put it, "Kundalini is God moving through your body." Each visitation was a moment of holy embrace.

Half the world (the West) had spent eons in an effort to expel this principle from awareness (the body is evil, feeling is bad, pleasure is sin). The other half (the East) had, in turn, passed centuries keeping such knowledge alive, though through the years awareness had filtered down to a constantly dwindling band.

Who knows but that a cat in its meditation, a turtle in the sunlight, or a rock contemplating the cliff to which it clings, is not, inwardly, quietly thrilling to universal currents which flow through it in streams of delight?

If we have fallen from God, perhaps it is in this: it is not that our minds or characters have been debased, but rather that our bodies—our airy, electric, radiant selves—have been cut off from the Source.

> How do you know but every Bird
> that cuts the airy way
> Is an immense world of delight,
> clos'd by your senses five?
>
> William Blake, *The Marriage of Heaven and Hell*

We are brought into a deceptive ego/identity so that we may learn what we are not. How do we discover that which we are?

All the world is seeking something it has lost, though most do not even realize what it is they seek. They look to things—gadgets,

machines, items—or to superficial human encounters, or point-
less occupations, to fill their lack. What they seek is of the spirit,
but they, denying spirit, cannot comprehend its absence, or ways
to recapture it.

In desperation, some turn to a debased Christianity of the modern mode. There they learn that "God is Hate" (the "fundamen-
talists," obsessed with "sin") or "God is Good Fellowship" (a
diluted humanism). Almost nowhere do they learn that God is Self,
spirit in matter, reality in temporality. Nowhere do they find how to
be lifted in an absolute sense, to experience actual transcendence.

*After the first weeks my subsequent efforts to rouse kundalini
were not always successful. Sometimes the "snake" bit its channel
only part way upward, and only feeble energies were roused in the
head. The experience became strain without satisfaction. Vague
nervous impulses pulsated briefly in neck or hand. My entire nervous system seemed out of balance. Therefore I sought a new technique (Transcendental Meditation), and in doing so, I stepped off
my true, inner directed path.*

*My initiation into TM was beautiful. Colors began to appear
sharper, more vivid. But soon both my body and my subconscious
mind began to rebel, to warn of my serious blunder in submitting
to an inappropriate external authority, one which seemingly elim-
inated body from consideration, and sought only pacification of
the being through quiet mind. I dutifully sat in meditation posture, repeating my assigned mantra, but it was as if a lid had been
placed on a vessel whose contents were boiling.*

Some Recent Dreams of Deception

I am on a car lot. The female salesperson is going to show me
two new models. While she is gone, I remember I have a good
older car at home. The new ones will be flashy and maybe flimsy.
Am I wise to change?

Interpretation: The salesperson is female. She could repre-
sent either S. (who is trying to "sell" me TM) or A., my therapist
friend who follows Bhagwan. Both of these systems offer updated,

revised versions of older spiritual modes. But do they have any real substance to them? My "older model" may be more substantial. Maybe I should stay with it. The "older model" could be either the ancient tradition I have contacted, or the summation of my life's spiritual search, that is, me.

I am riding a motor scooter, behind a man and a woman. She can hold on to him, but I have nothing to hold on to. Thus every time we start up, I bend backward, almost touching the ground. Finally, I am able to pull myself up, but with difficulty.

I keep my balance, but they go as fast as possible. There are other scooters and riders also. Then the ride is over. I walk away and discover I have on the wrong shoes. I go back to find the woman, and discover that she has my shoes. The ones I am wearing are those which are special for riding scooters. Then a little old man, very dark and wizened, a "foreigner" of some sort, is waiting to sell me something. (I had "looked over" his stuff before.) He sees me coming, and moves his car to make a place for me to park (I'm in my own big car now). My car keys get caught on a board (of keys). He pretends to locate them when I can't. Then he offers me a bracelet instead. It is a little present, a lure to get me to purchase the "expensive goods."

Interpretation: TM is called the "fast way" to enlightenment. The scooter riders may be S. and her husband, also a TM teacher. They "scoot" to heaven—in a way that is almost too powerful for me. The shoes have a special association with S. She often wears "odd" (rather flashy) shoes and stockings. I am wearing "borrowed shoes" (a false identity) for this occasion.

The old man may be Maharishi, who offers a "clever sell." He gives me something trivial (a simple meditation technique) in hopes that I will buy the larger package (the whole philosophy of TM). I don't buy it. Note the confusion of "his key" (his key board) with "my key" (my way). Clearly I am struggling here with a sense of having been sold a package of goods; I feel that I am in danger of trading something of great value for something that is of little or no value to me. I wonder if I shouldn't simply continue with the identity (belief system, techniques) I already have.

I am at the house of Carol (a close friend and colleague). Perhaps there has been a party. Another friend is there, apparently helping to pick up. I then find myself in Carol's arms. While she holds me, I feel nothing, either positive or negative. I discover that I can see with my eyes closed. I see the room we are in in some detail. Also, I see the next room. When I open my eyes (in the dream), I first think that I am mistaken—I am not sure that I saw this room that I am now in. Then I realize that I am looking at a second room (a bedroom) and that I had seen it also in my "blind vision." This proves that I really "saw with my eyes closed."

Interpretation: Carol is a person of powerful energies. Properly transmitted (with *no* feeling on my part of positive or negative—no judgment or personal response), they will empower me to see what I have not seen before.

Summary: If all of the characters are me (as some dream theory asserts), then, in the first dream, some part of myself is trying to sell another part something. There is considerable skepticism and uncertainty about what is actually going on. Are the goods I am considering (the new approach to spirituality) bright but shoddy (the cars on the lot)? Is the whole thing a con game (the old man of the second dream)? Carol is that aspect of *myself* that is wise, knowing, perceptive. If I will let this come through, without prejudging or predetermining how it should be, then I can "see through blindness." I can see the "room I am in" (where I am now) and rooms where I am not (the future, other realms of being). The new car, the ride on the motor scooter—these are not for me. I must draw on my own energies. Be who I am.

All of this reminds me of a dream I had last fall. First, I dreamt of a head that was quickly severed by a knife at the throat in a quick, bloodless cut. Then I dreamt of a head (more like a geometrical figure than a real cranium) with one-fourth of it missing—one of the upper quadrants simply was not there. These may be warnings of an impending stroke or possibly the danger of "losing your head," "losing the capacity to think for yourself." They may be urgent warnings against being sucked into a system not suited for me, such as TM.

My headaches, which had begun with the switch to the technique of Transcendental Meditation, were now increasing in an alarming way. Since I had never suffered such intense headaches before, my doctor advised a CAT scan to check for possible brain tumor. Fortunately, the test revealed nothing abnormal. After the morning of the scan, Kate and I went shopping, and everyone in the mall looked flushed with beauty.

Barriers Dissolving

They speak of the "opening" of the heart chakra. I have felt no such experience in my body. Yet more and more, love operates to dissolve all barriers between self and other, the internal and the external.

First, it was landscape. There were, of course, early (childhood) experiences of oneness—awe of nature, of woods, of mountain views, of still lakes. Later, before going to England in 1976, I found everything—trees, walls, streets—beautiful. And in London, also, colors, images, things of all sorts often became radiant, as if lit from within. Only later did I experience this effect with faces. At Lindisfarne, in my class years ago and again last fall, the people in the shopping mall recently—all seemed to glow with a transcendent luminosity, and I and they seemed one.

Yesterday, seated with three friends at lunch, I saw their inner beauty, felt the oneness of the group. First, I gazed at M., perhaps the most perfect human specimen (as far as physical beauty of face, hair, and teeth) that I have seen. I was marveling at her loveliness, when, suddenly, I "shifted," and the others were also caught in the shining net, each a perfection. One is somewhat overweight, a bleached blonde with flamboyant red lipstick—yet she was perfect, as were the others. I realized that, indeed, it was not a matter of the physical features or of the personality. It was the essential, beautiful divinity of spirit shining forth. The face was lit by the soul. The barriers dissolved, we were a "psychic unit" bonded in love. I loved, without reservation, saw each person in the light of her own profoundest beauty. In this state, traits

Unmasking the Rose

of personality or temperament become irrelevant. It is the divine
loveliness of the spirit which I perceive and merge with.

My Eleventh Year

More and more, I contemplate my eleventh year, and think it
has something to do with my present life. I think of solitary bicy-
cle rides down shaded country roads; the heady delight of an
unexpected snow in late April; the joy of cutting the water with
my child's body, arms flailing; the wonder of fields and woods. I
was, then, often in a state of elevated consciousness; such a state
may be normal for children, but most outgrow it all too soon.

Now I rediscover and *reaffirm* a nature always present, but
realized finally at its deeper level. It does not bother me to see
auras, feel another's subtle energy, or fall into psychic union with
others. These states are merely the deepening and intensification
of what I have always known and been.

The aura I see is now always a shade of purple. What is this?
How is it I see this color and not others? Do I respond only to
another's spirituality? (I associate purple with spiritual essence.)

Returning from *Samadhi*

When we first return from *samadhi,* it is not known whether
we are merely that which we were before the event (the
unchanged traveler), or whether we are truly transformed. The
first adjustment is one of condensation. During the episode, the
bliss, we experienced ourselves as air, as a space through which
reality poured, infusing us with its essence. Our molecules no
longer clustered about a fixed personal axis, but were dissolved
and diffused, permeated with energies irradiating us with their
own sweet necessities. A fragment of self-identity remained—we
were the atom shot with light but recognizable, the grain of salt
at the moment before it loses itself forever in the fluid.

And then we drew back. The atom shook itself, took on its customary unlit contours. The grain recovered its sense of separate

100

being, and pulled away at the critical moment. What had been rarefied was now compressed into a palpable mass, with boundaries, separation, extension in space and time. We are left to pick up our memory and begin again.

Yet we are haunted by uncertainty. Was the vision a reality, or a momentary aberration of an unbalanced psyche? What is the relation of this ordinary self with its catalogue of physical defects, its disgruntled spirit, its nagging desire for improvements to the awareness which so briefly centered in the eternal? How can we cope with a world of differences, of separations, when we have been bathed in oneness?

Occasionally, a curtain lifts, and we are permitted brief reminders of our (by now) vaguely recollected transcendence. A piece of music lifts us out of ourselves, a tree arises commandingly in consciousness, the faces of friends suddenly take on a luminosity almost unbearable in its intensity. "Why," we say to ourselves, "anyone can be an angel. Everywhere is paradise. Immanence and transcendence, nirvana in samsara—these words carry meaning after all."

But such moments are rare, and tease us into longing for the pure experience which is not an interval but an unbroken extension.

Is death then a light that does not go out, a line that does not end?

Not Ecstasy, but Peace

This, then, is the turning, the confrontation with the final phase. What we seek now is not ecstasy, but peace, not euphoric oneness with all but freedom from the aches and pains that assault us daily.

A Flame in Whose Center I Stood

When I think of the experiences of a year ago, I might as well try to describe a flame in whose center I stood and was not consumed. What powered me then was not of the present life's dimension.

What animates me now is not of that other's plane. Kundalini—Western science has yet to tell us what it is, how it operates. Is it merely thought expressing itself in unfamiliar ways within the body? Or is it, truly, an energy-force as yet unknown and unnamed?

To have this experience was like being shot as a skyrocket into space, there to bloom in bursts of fire, falling, falling, through unknown space. Where I landed may be at a place lower than where I began. Nonetheless, through effort, through persistent trial, I labor back toward the point of my original departure, which has, of course, now disappeared forever. Whatever it was, it was the focal point, "the center toward which all things converged, the point from which all things thereafter flowed."

Who Move Among Us

At midnight
in silence
we press
the dark oil
of our life's meaning
from a hundred nights of pain,
limitless days of dying.

What is joy
if not union
with the god
or else unbearable intensity of longing?
What is sorrow
but a glance imploring
that silent face?

Angels, I know you move
constantly among us
your stirring wings, your soft embrace—
we sense your nearness . . .
how can we withstand
such blood driven tokens
of your insistent claim?

Part 3

In Ecstasy and Humiliation

Ruined by Your Beauty

First, you cleansed me,
arriving as fire, as savage flood.

Next you tore me,
your panther tooth,
your lion claw,
limbs scattering like grass
in the garden of a great wind.

Then you made love to me,
night after night of unendurable
torment and passion.

Ruined by your beauty,
I have vanished,
fled into the nothingness
of who I am.

St. John of the Cross

Saint John compares the practice of contemplation to a ladder of ten steps, "which the soul is ascending and descending continually in ecstasy and humiliation until it has acquired perfect habits."

> I groaned; "Be quiet," he said.
> I was quiet: he said, "Groan!"
> I grew feverish: he said, "Be calm!"
> I grew calm; he said, "I want you to burn."

Rumi, translated by Andrew Harvey

Now I continued the long slow process of balancing and integration, during which sensitivity to both pleasure and pain were dramatically heightened.

Taking on Another's Vibrations

Brugh Joy warns against taking on another's vibrations, another's problems. Indeed, this can be devastating.

This morning, I attended a ceremony closing a drive for the Equal Rights Amendment. I saw my colleague there (the one whose face had appeared superimposed over mine in the mirror) and concentrated on sending her love. But afterward, I had a sense of agonizing pinpricks all over my body. Some time ago, I was telling another friend at lunch how much I was enjoying my meditations. At the very moment I spoke, I developed a severe backache, the ailment of which she complained. Another time, a student came to my office with a serious personal problem of some sort. I developed a headache so intense I had to go home. Thus I often "pick up" others' disturbances. When I do yoga, and other practices, I feel better for a time. But even as I write this, I feel the strange "prickling."

On Tuesday (the day before yesterday), I visited with a new friend, who has attended workshops with Brugh Joy and who is deeply engaged in energy work. She saw my aura as green, which she associated with the heart and healing. I saw her aura as a vivid hue of violet. Its brightness was appropriate to her health and vitality. She scanned my chakras, and said that the throat and sex chakras were the strongest. I felt her heart chakra as heat, extending up into my forearm as well as my hands. She thought I should be able to sense her energies when she was scanning me (in "my space"), and maybe I did a little. Joy says that the throat and sex chakras are a pair that "open together naturally." He associates the throat with speech, language, and various artistic and psychic activities.

Curious Dreams

A recent dream of a past life, in which I saw myself as the mother of a child who had killed another child, seems to connect with an earlier one in which I identified with the "widower," the "good man" of a rough city neighborhood, who had lost his son to the neighborhood tough. Thus, I experience both roles—parent of the victim, parent of the incorrigible child. Both undergo acute suffering, brought on by the action of another, for whom one both is and is not responsible.

If the person in this recent dream is me then this perhaps may explain why I have never considered having children. *Perhaps* it accounts for some of the guilt I have carried since childhood (guilt for a deed I did not do.) Or perhaps it explains *why* I "came through," even when my mother thought to abort me.

Here is another dream of several nights ago: First, I experienced a sensation in the lower chakras, a feeling which was strong and sexual in tone. Then it was "brought up", as if transformed, into a nonsexual feeling. Then it went back to its original state as a sexual impulse, and then again it rose as a "neutral" feeling. The purpose of this was, I felt, to demonstrate the range and relation of sexual and nonsexual impulses. It was a practical illustration of the transformation of energies which is sometimes done consciously, often not.

Kundalini Is a Mixed Experience

Kundalini—we long for a single, permanent, everlasting experience of it. We yearn to be established once and forever in the center of bliss, to carry with us always our own perpetual radiance, to illumine and enlighten wherever we go.

But this, like all human experiences, is mixed. We falter, we lose "control" (which is by way of not controlling). Our energies go awry, we feel pain where before we sensed ecstasy. Negative energies assault the head, health begins to fail.

But then, just as we are about to conclude that we have merely stumbled on an illusion, an aberration produced by unsteady nerves or an unbalanced constitution, we experience a day like the day of the awakening. Only, now feelings are toned down, modified. Our sensations are spontaneous, neither begotten of mental images or energies awakened during sleep, nor aroused by our conscious intent. We move innocently through our asanas, and the "raptures" come. But they are tempered, modified to our body's capacity to receive. Our eyes, our cheeks, our lips (as well as arms, legs, hands, toes) are bathed in ecstasy. In this condition, we execute a sacred dance, where every movement is a rapture, every turning a bliss.

Last year was one of upheaval, of radical assault and violent transformation on all levels. This year is a time of integration, of quiet assimilation of the many changes and inner conversions that have occurred.

Perhaps today's experiences seemed mild mainly because they were familiar. Had such feelings come as new experience, they might have set in motion the same train of events as took place a year ago. How was this present reversal (to a feeling level, which is, however, "bearable bliss") produced? By abandoning conscious intention to rouse kundalini. By deciding to opt for purity, right living, higher consciousness. By deciding to let kundalini come if it would, but by its own intention, not mine. Once this decision was made (last night), the headache cleared, the eyes relaxed, and the body tone was good. Today, I feel wonderful, in body and spirit.

Balancing Energies

On Thursday morning, at 11 A.M., Susan (Brugh Joy's student) balanced my energies. She brought with her Ruth, a friend from out of town.

I lay on the long coffee table in the living room. Susan first had all of us meditate to center and focus on the ceremonies. During the balancing, Susan usually kept one hand on my shoulder. (Or was it my waist?) She moved the other hand above my body at various places, to bring the energies into harmony. I kept my eyes shut during the procedure. I kept thinking I could watch the process later, when Susan worked on her friend. I felt relatively little while she was working on me. But at the end, when Susan placed both hands over my heart, I felt a great surge of delightful energy in the chest. I wanted to lift out of my body completely, or else to levitate.

I sat up quickly after it was over, and announced that I wasn't all that "out of it." I moved to a chair by the record cabinet while Susan began to balance Ruth. I closed my eyes and immediately fell into intense ecstasy. I could not even open my eyes to watch the balancing of Ruth.

Near the end, Susan invited me to check Ruth's chakras, to see if they were balanced. I ran my hands over (above) Ruth's body. Actually, I felt nothing, but I acted as if I did, since that seemed to be expected. Then, Susan told me to take Ruth's feet. Susan took her head. The energy was supposed to flow between us. From the moment I took the feet, I felt strong waves of delightful energy surge into my hands and body. I almost shook with the power of the vibrations.

When it was finished, Ruth sat up, looked at me, and said, "You have incredible power in your hands." She said that she "had never felt anything like it before." When I asked her to describe it, she said it was "ecstasy."

Scanning

I am becoming even more sensitive to the energies of other people. Sunday night, I "scanned" various friends, by running my hands over (above) their bodies to see if their energies were flowing evenly. I had scanned Dana earlier. She said that while I did this, she felt energy move in her spine. When I scanned Kate, she looked ecstatic. She said my hands felt like a cross between air and water—as if "something were being rubbed over her skin." Her cheeks, in particular, felt the effect. I also scanned Brad and Pat, two gay male friends. I felt warmth in Brad's solar plexus, and in Pat's throat. Neither felt any energy from me.

Increased sensitivity to energies of many kinds is commonly experienced by those with awakened kundalini.

The Balancing of Dana

I did yoga to music in preparation for the balancing of Dana, a young friend. From the first movement in *asana,* I felt ecstatic energy begin to build in my body. I concentrated on my upper torso, arms, and hands, since I felt these would be most important for the balancing procedure. I think I danced in ecstasy, particularly aware of delightful feeling in my hands.

At first, I scanned her. Her heart chakra felt very strong. Also her head—in fact, almost all of her centers were intense (I noted this even more on the next round—the balancing itself). I began, according to Joy's recommendation, with the right ankle and knee. I touched each with a hand. Susan said we should "wait for a sign" to tell us when to go on. She did not say what this would be. By now I was feeling high ecstasy in my body.

I touched Dana's ankle and knee and waited. Soon I felt a surge of ecstatic feeling flowing up one arm, through the head, and down the other arm. It was as if an electric circuit had been closed and energy pulsed through. I then went to the next position—right knee and hip. The same thing happened here, a "charge" moving up the arm, through the head, and down the other arm and hand. The same thing happened in all but one or two positions. Once, I had to switch to the left side of Dana's body to reach her left upper arm and I had some difficulty—also I think I got no charge from her shoulders.

When I tried to locate the end of her "transpersonal point" (the energy that radiates outward from the head), I could not find the end of it: I felt warmth extending four to five feet beyond her crown, and decided that the rest of it must go on outside somewhere. When I "connected" here, I again felt a charge, but only in the hand that was on her head. The "observing" friend said that she was able to feel my energy when I was working on Dana's head.

Early on, I had become extremely hot—my hands, face, and entire body were burning. Twice I had to go out to get water, and Susan said I should never do this when I was alone with a "client."

So, the significant features of the experience were ecstasy, my inner heat, and the connecting charges. Also, the fact that I could actually sense Dana's energies as heat, and could feel it in my forearms and even elbows as well as my hands. My responses were, I felt, all a consequence of my own recent awakening.

After we finished, Dana described her experiences. She had seen images of "fairies dancing." These were creatures of human height with flowing garments and transparent bodies. Susan received images of pyramids and a sphinx. I received only one brief image, and that occurred when I was over the root chakra. I immediately brushed it aside, as it seemed to be phallic, and hence inappropriate: it was the kundalini symbol, the snake curled around the phallic stone.

I was extremely tired later—perhaps I gave too much of my own energy. But today (the day after) I feel excellent, as if I had done the thing I needed to do, as if this was the goal I sought, as if I was finally comfortable with the energy. However, today at lunch I again had "pain in the head" after a morning of bliss.

This morning during yoga, I felt my heart included in the upper resonance centers (head, arms, chest). It is becoming more blissful, though not as fully sensitized as the other centers. This morning, I "broke" the connection with several persons who were important in my past and with whom I still felt deep emotional ties. I did this by playing music that I associated with them.

I thought of my friend who died recently, and how she seemed to be connected with all this somehow, as if she were giving me a gratuitous gift to make amends for past indifference. Or perhaps merely from unconditional love. I sent mental love to my mother, also a major influence (and contributor of vibrations). I need to go to see my mother soon. Today is Bastille Day, her birthday. She is now eighty-five years old, generally weak and feeble.

What Is this Ecstasy?

Here is the routine: we lie down on our back each morning to do yoga. We feel intense, sensual energy. We turn over on our stomach. There is more energy. We do yoga. We dance. Energy becomes ecstasy. What is this energy? What is this ecstasy? Who is this dancer?

A Spirit Cat Appears

Yesterday evening, Kate and I had supper with a friend, an "Emissary of Divine Light," who "shares attunements" with us— energy balancing, in other words. We were at her house. During the evening, a young couple from her group dropped in with a child. I noticed good clear vibrations from him—also from the child later. Then the couple left. As our friend was speaking, I saw purple light play around her face and shoulders, all of her upper body, in fact.

On the way home, I thought of M. Kabal. How different our present spiritual experience is from that earlier episode. I recalled how that was essentially a union stressing psychic power and poetic creativity, and that this stresses the spiritual element. I considered how I would surely progress into the practice of healing through the techniques of this or some similar group.

At home later, Kate came into the living room from the bathroom and announced, matter-of-factly: "Well, we have a black cat." She said that she had seen it clearly in the hall mirror while she was washing her hands. She said it seemed as real as any of the others (the two who live with us). She knew it was a "spirit cat" only because we do not in fact have a black cat, only two tiger stripes. Further, it was large, fluffy, imperious—clearly a male (ours are female, and rather small). It was not at all interested in her. She simply had seen its reflection in the mirror as it passed by. I then told her the story taken from Yeats of the person who

saw a spectral cat in the corner; he finally decided to get rid of it
and did so by tossing it out the window.

Later, as we were getting ready for bed, I teased Kate (she is
a great lover of animals): "This is just like you to come up with
something like this. Who else would 'materialize' an animal?"
Then, just as I was drifting off to sleep, I thought of the cat again.
I think I was going over the details of her account in my mind
when the cat spoke in her sleep.

Her voice (the voice that spoke through her) was very controlled, firm, and adult. This is clearly a being to be reckoned
with. He is very commanding, not threatening, but one would not
wish to dispute his authority.

"I *am* a black cat who lives with you."

Why are you here?

"I am a guardian. . . of divine wisdom. You have summoned
me."

Which of us has summoned you?

"Do you mean *both* or just you?"

Yes.

"Mainly you . . . but also Kate to some extent."

What is your name?

"Akramis." (ahk-rah-mis)

How do you spell it?

"*You* would spell it A-k-r-a-m-i-s. . . . I serve the high priestess
Rami." (ray-mee)

What does your name mean?

"That is not important. . . ."

Is it taken from Rami?

"Yes."

Are you from Egypt?

"That is for me. . . . We serve Isis."

What will you do for us?

"That is for me. . . . I will be here in case you need me."

How long have you been here?

"Remember. . . . One calls me. I am substanced in the mind
of the other."

This, as best as I can remember, is last night's message. After the voice spoke (through Kate), I thought of getting up to write the message down. I felt I should not leave her, though. While I was debating (some minutes after), Kate turned, still asleep, and linked her arm around mine, holding me down. She then asked me in a young child's voice if an arm could be squared, and went off into some "nonsense" about positive numbers and negatives. She thought that it (the arm) could be squared because it was real.

Before I went to sleep, I was thinking I would never see the cat, only Kate would. I felt that either Kate alone would see the cat, or that Kate alone would perceive divine wisdom. Yet, I realize that through her I will also be drawn to it and experience it. I will witness and observe through her. Through her mind the wisdom will manifest. Both energies are necessary; both beings are required. Together we form a unit of reception and perception, together they are one. Receiver and witness.

Attunements

Next day I saw many auras of purplish light around faces, especially at lunch. I seemed to see a more complete aura (white light overarched by a delicate "rainbow") over one student. Also, I seemed to see a funnel (of dim yellowish, orangish hue) entering another's crown (again, my TM teacher).

I had arranged for Arlene to come to the Women's Studies office over the noon hour, where we would offer free "attunements" for anyone who was interested. I hoped to learn the technique from working with her. On Tuesday, we had our first session. First, Arlene worked on the head of the client; then I joined her, pointing my closed fingers at her feet, and immediately felt a delightful flow of energy in my hands and up into my forearms as far as my elbows. I also sensed some energy in the head. Then Arlene warned me not to allow the energy anywhere but in my hands, because it could be harmful. The client said that she had felt an increase of energy when I joined the "attunement."

Of late, people, as well as natural scenery, appear very beautiful. All come through as if radiating their highest perfection. They literally have "shining faces." (Arlene says that I am seeing the "angel" in them.)

Today, Kate and Arlene went to a nearby state to the farm and lands owned by A.'s group. Kate called and said they would "share an attunement" with me long-distance at 8:45. I actually felt it beginning about two or three minutes early. It was very powerful: sweet energy flowing in and around my head—especially my eyes, and my neck. There was a sense of the opening of the head. Also, I felt cool energies flowing all through my body. The experience lasted about fifteen minutes.

Q. What is this?
A. *(from the inner voice)* This is cosmic energy. The flowing force of the divine. It is unsubstanced reality charging matter with vitality, giving life to the unliving, quickening that which is inert. It is your why, your wherefrom, your self. It is Being. (Which you can participate but never adequately define.)

A Fall

On Saturday around noon, I had a fall, while I was attending an out-of-town conference. Apparently I failed to see a curb, and I pitched headfirst onto the concrete. I did not lose consciousness. I felt no pain, but I was extremely disoriented, or, possibly, lacking in orientation, since for a few seconds I seemed only obscurely aware of what had happened, who I was, where, and so on. I lay still for some time, spread-eagled in the parking lot, wondering what damage had been done. Kate, who was nearby but had not seen me fall, thought I had had a heart attack or stroke. When I finally raised my head, the sight, apparently, was shocking. My face was smeared with blood and mud; my nose was beginning to swell. We made a stop at the emergency room of the local hospital. I washed my face and got a tetanus shot. They said I would have to wait for two or three days to see if my nose was broken.

Kate and I returned home that afternoon. I stayed in for the next three days, applying much vitamin E to my bruises. On Monday, I felt "fluish." I had a slight case of fever and chills, possibly from the tetanus shot. On Tuesday I felt better; my head cleared and I wrote a paper for delivery later this month.

Certain events proceed in a pattern up to and away from this incident:

Foremost is the resignation of the dean I have worked for so many years, the one I respect so much. He was forced out of office by university politics. I grieved his going deeply. During this period, I found myself awakening at night and vomiting. I ask, can good *never* triumph in the struggle with evil (an exaggeration, but nonetheless, my feeling at the time). On Thursday, before we left for the conference, I attended his farewell meeting with the chairs of the departments and the humanities faculty. I noted that everyone looked beautiful. I was deeply moved.

At the conference, on Friday and Saturday, again everyone and everything looked beautiful during the meetings. I realized that I was in a slightly altered state. I left before the political fireworks erupted. I realized I was getting too excited. On Saturday, after my accident, I again saw the world as beautiful. Coming home, I shut my eyes and saw small spots of brilliant color; often, one color surrounded another.

Then, by Tuesday, my head cleared. For the last several days, yoga ecstasy has been good but it is more refined than previously. I tried certain breathing exercises, alternating left and right nostrils, and felt exquisite sensations within the nose. It was delicate but intensely sensuous. I could only bear to do this three or four times. Also, even when I simply breathe when meditating or doing *asanas,* I feel a delicate ecstasy. I feel as though I have at last found how to contact *prana,* that this is the lifting of energy into the "higher" chakras. The sensations are infinitely subtle, delightful, thrilling, a gentle ecstasy, as if this is the combination of "ecstasy" and "tranquillity" I had sought.

My nervous system is more sensitive, but I am at the same time more grounded, more solid. I had more physical energy this weekend approaching (though not matching) that of the experience of two years ago. Perhaps something was made okay by the fall. Perhaps some needed physical adjustment occurred.

For over a year, I have had a series of peculiar physical symptoms that have followed one after another, all essentially "new" to my system. First came the severe backaches after I started TM. To curb the back pain, I took hormones for two months. Throughout the spring, I developed incredible headaches of migraine intensity. I asked to have my blood sugar level checked, and I was pronounced diabetic. Finally, after I had a CAT scan to see if I had a brain tumor (negative), I gave up on TM as a meditation technique, and the headaches gradually cleared. From time to time, particularly when under stress, I had a sensation of pinpricks, or little stabbing pains in random flashes over my body. An eye infection lasted for many weeks during the summer, and there was much "inner trembling," especially in the head. Here, there, everywhere were problems.

I was generally feeling good by the end of summer, but after the pressure of an intense writing project of last fall, I developed new symptoms. I had much racing heart, ultimately chest pains, especially at night. Even before these started, I had had much itching and tingling in the region of the heart. Then about one month ago, I had violent upper stomach cramps and even vomiting, especially when I tried to drink milk. Always, there is a loud ringing in my head, and much peculiar tingling or vibration in my hands, feet, legs. *All of these are commonly occurring symptoms of persons undergoing kundalini awakening. Many other negative reactions may also manifest. Apparently, as the energy moves through the system, it encounters various blocks, physical, emotional, or psychological. When its progress is impeded, physical or psychological distress may ensue. A widely held belief is that these signs of illness or disturbance will disappear once the system is purified and balance has been restored.*

In any event, I feel well, energized, as of last week. Perhaps something that needed to happen did happen. Something received a jolt, a shock. I had been reading about the prostration position shortly before my fall, and thought that I would not try to do the 200,000 obeisances, or whatever the number is. Perhaps my one traumatic fall was the equivalent of many such voluntary prostrations. The ultimate effect was that of an electric shock clearing a system. Was it accidental or planned?

Within a week, my wounds have all but healed, possibly because of the vitamin E. My initial appearance, with a scar down my nose, suggested a "lightning flash" etched on my countenance. The streak was amazingly centered. I joked to myself that this must be the "lightning flash" of enlightenment. In appearance, I reminded myself of a Picasso painting. Now the scar is not nearly so conspicuous.

The beauty of the ordinary is my current theme. I am intrigued by the mundane, either external seeing or internal sensation. For this I am grateful. I have come down from the mountain, only to find the beauty at the bottom rivals (indeed, is the same beauty) as that at the top. I am enamored and even thrilled by familiar objects and commonplace events, but I am no longer swept away by my perceptions.

A Place Where a Hurricane Has Passed

Still, no ecstasy, but no frazzled nerves. On the one hand, there is a huge relief; perhaps a process, begun two years ago, has finally played itself out, run down. On the other hand, one wonders a little: is this a sign of a "fall from grace," a failure of the self to maintain the necessary state for favor to descend? Well, no matter. What is important is the securing of full health, of restoration of energy, of replenishment of vitality. I wonder if I ever had diabetes at all. I now have a blood sugar reading of 106, declared to be normal. The earlier reading was 112, and it was pronounced abnormal. Perhaps my symptoms were of the nerves rather than of the blood or cells.

In some respects, I feel like a place a hurricane has passed over. Repairs have been made, damage is mainly concealed—yet somewhere, in the throb of root or the Earth, there is a deep memory, a knowledge that vibrates, suffusing the scene with its recollection of that which it has been and therefore is.

Three years ago, there was heat (the summer weather) and language (writing); two years ago, ecstasy; a year ago, a weakness as of some part or organ which was ill; and now, there is waiting, a pause to catch a new direction or set a course.

In Balance

By now, the heavy ecstasy of the earlier times is dissipated. There is, rather, a stimulating of gentler energies which suffuse the body. At times, they are barely distinguishable from those ordinary states called "feeling good." Something has smoothed out, balanced, come to its center. Sometimes I even feel these soft waves of well-being while walking or moving about.

In any event, it took two years. In that time I weathered the onset of menopause, with its many accompanying discomforts, which were often similar to those of the kundalini process; infidelity; a spontaneous kundalini rising; parental illness, and other things. No wonder my health suffered. Any one of these could produce acute physical distress. But now "diabetes," nerves, domestic life all seem under control.

Touch Therapy

For the past week, I have had a slight headache, felt pressure in the head plus various aches in my hands and feet. The discomfort has the same tone as that following my fall, as if the nerves were ill, traumatized. Two or three days ago, I even had painful vibrations in my teeth (or at least in the gums). It was brief, one or two shudders like a slight electric shock in the mouth. It was as if I had bitten into metal, or something too cold. This is going too far, I thought. And I wondered if I had a gum disorder.

Last night, I awoke about 2 A.M. and got up to put on the air-conditioning. When I lay back down, I decided to apply gentle pressure to my neck vertebra to see if it helped ease my overall achiness. I felt *immediate* release, relaxation, and sweet flowing energies in the area I had touched. I moved up to the next vertebra. Gentle pressure produced the same effect. I then tried others, always with the same effect.

Next morning, I touched the crown; then, I went down the front of my body. For two hours I did this and felt delightful energy flow with each location (with perhaps one or two exceptions—there was one hard place on the skull below the crown, and one place on the forehead that yielded no response). It was a deeply healing experience. I realized it was not just the position and pressure per se, but the literal flow of energy from my hands that produced the release. It was "healing energy" that produced a sense of well-being.

Sweet Flowing Energy

Each day there is more sweet flowing energy from tai chi and yoga. As if I had dropped back and started again at the beginning, this time building more slowly, more cautiously. All from a few simple tai chi exercises (up and down, right and left, back and forward). All this to achieve balance, centering, and delight.

The Task That Is Most Difficult

Why is it that always, just when we think we are *about* to arrive, as we are ready to put our foot over the threshold, we are blocked? The brilliant landscape around us fades to a dingy brown, the seeming doorway rolls away, now revealed as a Hollywood prop on wheels.

On Sunday, after days of tai chi bliss and yogic ecstasy, when wondrous energies were flowing, when I felt I had at last "achieved mastery" of the techniques, I found, suddenly that I had a dancing film or net before my eye. Jagged filaments rushed across my plane of vision and floated back. My head grew tense, a center somewhere inside inflamed.

What is the cause of these sudden reversals? Will I never be established in balanced energy? Why does my body feel so cold much of the time?

For over a week, I have had no outdoor exercise because of the heat. Is this the cause of my seeming debility? Or is the weather itself—the 65 percent humidity, the hundred degree temperature—the cause? (Inside, the air conditioner keeps the house very cool.)

If we were certain all this led to an *outcome,* if we knew these were temporary discomforts to be passed through on our way to redemption, then all would be easy to bear. But we walk always on a tightly drawn rope, swaying now this way, now that, occasionally catching our balance and holding it for an interval as our body moves forward across the immeasurable chasm below.

Floaters

On Tuesday, I saw the ophthalmologist. He felt that my vision problem came from yoga. I had added one new exercise in which my head went far down in a standing position. Also, I had been doing the preliminary headstand for about two weeks. Apparently, this was dangerous for me, given my age and extreme myopia. Something in my eye gave way, some fluid came forward to the front, and now I have floaters. They will probably be with me for a long time—years, in fact.

It seems that by trying to improve my health, I damage it. By eliminating meat from my diet (and including more starches), I acquire diabetes. By overdoing yoga, I lose some of my capacity for seeing. I watch myself aging at an accelerated pace, despite the claims of the various systems to invigorate and rejuvenate. Just when we think all is finally in balance, we fail. And when we are about to give up entirely, we are restored. At whose direction or command?

The Right Path at Last

Yesterday and today, I experienced much deep ecstasy—of movement, of breathing, of merely being still. Surely I have found the right path at last.

Another Superb Meditation

On Sunday, I had another superb meditation with much circulation of prana. Today, I had good breathing during meditation and yoga. I decided to see if I could continue to circulate prana all day. About noon I sat down to "breathe." Before I knew it, kundalini was flowing up the spine—the sensations became intense and finally exquisite. It was almost a repetition of the initial experience, but somewhat lessened in intensity especially in the head, where I felt only a mild sensation.

After the first intense ecstasy, I took two short recesses, and each was followed by an exquisite kundalini experience. Then I danced, still in rapture.

The timing here (just before the beginning of the fall semester) suggests that my psyche wishes to do as much as possible before work pressures begin again. It is as if there are certain stages to be passed along the way, certain "graduation ceremonies" to be experienced with these stages.

Changing Pain to Pleasure

This morning, I decided not to seek any ecstasy since I had had such intense experiences yesterday. I was doing a few tai chi exercises when I was interrupted by B., who needed help with his painting and repair work. While I was helping him unstick windows (mostly I was just standing inside, ready to report if one would open), I was seized with pain in the abdomen that felt much like the colon spasm I have had many times in the past.

A few minutes later, when I was alone, I took two calcium pills and began to press and massage my abdomen and lower back. But the pain persisted. I decided to "think away" the pain but had little success. It then occurred to me to *change the pain to pleasure*. I began to "allow" pleasure to come to consciousness. Immediately, the pain subsided and kundalini ecstasy began. It lasted about one hour—I felt it very strongly in the lower chakras, but to some extent (rather strong, in fact) in the upper body and head. It was almost too intense to bear. How much ecstasy can one take? I seem to be finding out. But the experience is difficult to capture in language. How can one describe these totally subjective responses? How can one delineate the contours of any internal experience, such as a thrill or an agony? What is the origin of sensation? What sort of goddess defines herself as exquisite pleasure? Why does she transform to pain when she is thwarted? It is as though she must be released, must know herself fully as unimpeded bliss.

It was my friend Carol who, after reading this account, said that for such an event to occur here, in Kansas, the very center of Middle America, where knowledge of Eastern practice has not penetrated, was a cosmic joke. And to have it happen to someone who was not really "in touch" with groups or systems practicing this method—again, the work of a cosmic prankster.

Living without Language

Today, I did tai chi exercises for about twenty minutes, followed by about ten minutes of yoga. After that, I did "ecstatic breathing" (yoga breathing, filling from the abdomen) for about thirty minutes. Then I went for lunch at my therapist friend's house. During the time I was there, I felt myself "pulsating" with delight. Later, after I came home, I raised kundalini to the head twice more. Everything seems natural, easy, with no bad aftereffects. But what shall I do without words? My eyes do not allow me to do extensive reading. I have no great compulsion to write. My current project is intense feeling. What shall I *become* without language?

Notes toward a Scenario for a Possible Future

I now began to reflect on the contours of an ideal future world.

- The future will not be like the past.

- Its full contours—its ultimate shape and nature—cannot be known.

- Its discoveries will be at once new and old, revelatory and restorative, unexpected and familiar.

- It will be based on extremely simple principles. Simplicity—of thought, attitude, and behavior—will be a key theme.

- It will work because it is self-validating.

Some Key Motifs

- The rediscovery of the sacred.

- Respect for diversity: of modes of illumination, formulations of thought, ways of acting out ideas, etc.

- Acceleration in time; the new consciousness will be contagious.

- Discovery of unlimited energy within the self.

- Infinite personal and communal bliss, from moments of joy to perpetual rapture.

Its Social Features

- Everyone will have a place in the new society.

- Everyone will have a sense of significant purpose—the reason to be is to enjoy being.

- Everyone will have meaningful work.

- There will be constant positive reinforcement through thought waves, good vibrations, constant exchange of positive energies.

- There will be continual excitement from the joy of discovery.

- There will be diversity of lifestyles, creeds, philosophies but all will share a common base.

- The bond between the human and the divine (the ultimate actual) will be reestablished.

- The spirit will be reunited with the body and the psyche.

Brainstorms of the Future

- Pollution will be filtered out by new life forms, or "purified" creatures (human, animals) now living.

- Help will come from acknowledged "supernatural" sources.

- Kundalini will play a primary role.

- Armaments, missiles, armies will not be banned but will be forgotten through disuse.

- Social deviates who threaten the good of the whole will be surrounded by a field of love and thus brought back to equilibrium.

- Stress itself will lay us open to illumination—an infusion of known but unrecognized realities.

- Telepathic communication between species.

- Open channels of communication with divine intelligence.

- Long-distance telepathic communication.

- Opening of the universal heart chakra.

- Massive kundalini experiences.

- Transformation of sex energy to higher energies.

The Transition Period:

- Those who have deliberately chosen incarnation at this time will act as centers of revitalization of society. They are marked by a sense of special purpose. Their aim is service, not self-aggrandizement.

- Some will remember themselves through gradual, ancient paths. Others will have a sharp awakening, to speed the transition.

- They will find one another, to give courage and strength.

- It will be a rough time—none will know if they are "chosen" or victims of mass delusion.

- The beginning will be the hardest; after the movement swells, progress will come more easily. The beginning will come at a time of universal darkness and despair.

- Many will say, "Nothing is possible," and abandon hope. Others, in transformation, will say, "If this is possible, anything is possible."

- After a slow beginning, this phenomenon will quickly spread.

At Last, Someone Who Has Had the Experience

It had now been over two years since my awakening. During this time, I had met no one who had experienced or who was familiar with kundalini. Hence I was excited to encounter someone who had gone through the transformation.

Recently, I attended a body workshop given by a visiting follower of Bhagwan Rajneesh (she is a friend of my therapist acquaintance who also follows Bhagwan). The workshop included many activities I have never participated in before, such as rapid breathing, free-form group dancing, and the laying on of hands. Early in the rapid breathing, I felt a deep sense of anguish, but I quickly stifled the feeling and held back the tears, since I did not wish to display emotion before others. Actually, I experienced a mixture of pleasure and pain during this exercise, and as for the rest, it was a continuous high, with much intense ecstatic feeling throughout.

During the week that followed, I had alternate days of ups and downs, pleasure and pain. It was as though the feeling of pain that had come up during the breathing exercise had not been released.

Afterwards, I talked with the leader of the workshop and she told me that she, too, had had a kundalini awakening. She was in Bhagwan's retreat in India when this occurred. She went into seclusion for several weeks, experiencing ecstasy for days on end. She went on a purification diet (I think I instinctively tried to do this), and later had illness or symptoms of illness. She now has one side of her body "turned on," while the other is "just normal." She knows a few other people who have had kundalini arousal. One was "a truck driver, or something like that," not a particularly "spiritual person." Another was a man who was extremely upset by having the experience, and was determined not to have it again.

A Bitter Snowstorm

A bitter snowstorm, temperatures plunge, and the world becomes a place of beauty and terror. The air is crystal-clear—a pre-pollution Eden. Yet always there is the lurking fear of imminent annihilation—if the car stalls and one waits too long for rescue, if one contracts bronchial disease from spending too long sweeping snow from car windows, from heat failure, water failure, or other crises. As if the benevolence that sustains the world has receded slightly, and a more hostile countenance has taken its place, almost taunting us with "What I could do if I wanted."

The Writer Versus the Mystic

The writer in me, given a chance, will snatch pen and paper, obsessively describe all states of being, from ecstasy to despair, whose formulations she has begun even in the midst of the experience. The mystic in me is easily lulled by her rapture into forgetfulness of all that is worded or expressed in symbol. Katherine Anne Porter speaks of the difference between mere adventure and real experience. Experience is the truth that finally overtakes you, she says.

A Sacred Bird

Sometime back, I dreamed of being visited by a sacred bird. Black, but with some colored plumage, she arrives at my door along with her young one. The youngster is smaller, similar in color, but not so brightly feathered. (I think perhaps the mother brings her chick with her to make sure I perceive her as female.) The mother bird has only one eye, and this is in the center of her forehead. She is about three feet tall, and her baby is about two feet.

People exclaim it is amazing she has come here because there are only 20 of them left in the world. She is real and sacred. I feel that it is indeed marvelous to have her appear like this. She stands in front of the door, waiting.

What Do We Seek?

I meet L., a student, at school today. As always, she draws me out, wants to know what is going on in my life. I try telling without telling, speaking without saying. Yet I give much of myself away.

Part of this reticence arises from the simultaneous longing for and fear of communication. We yearn to tell our story, to share our experience, yet we dread self-disclosure. Perhaps to speak is a mark of ego, a form of bragging, for being "special." Public revelation might violate the sacred quality of the experience. Maybe we feel that, to serve as an example, we ourselves need to draw nearer to perfection. Yes, says the inner voice, we went through this marvelous mystical adventure, our energy swelled, our faces bloomed, but then, we tripped and spiraled down, our flesh spotted and stretched, our hair drifted away from our skull, deep lines appeared on our face—who would wish to emulate such a flawed model? Disciples want young, firm, eager flesh, ardent spirits, inspirational beings. Can I embody my message?

What do we long for, what do we want, what do we dream of, what do we fear? Perhaps what we seek is this: an inner steadiness, a stable purity to cleanse and sanctify the matrix of self, a touch of the sacred. That which is holy seeks nothing more than to transform the dross to the pure, to lift the commonplace into the realm of the transcendent. Consciousness is the key, also the lock and door. One right turn, and our lives swing open upon eager hinges, pivoting at last toward that realm so long sought and desired. Once inside, we recognize it is the room where we were born, the place we have in fact never left. It is the site of our origin and end, our beginning and destination.

A New House

Last night I dreamed once again that I had moved to a new house with my parents. It is a large house, with several floors and rooms and wonderful unexpected spaces. I am delighted with it. One room, which is a kind of extension (added room), to an upper floor, contains furniture from my parents' present home. The furniture is dark, like their red mahogany pieces. I am enchanted with it. The bottom section of a dresser had been turned into a desk, which is beautifully carved, almost ornate. (As an adolescent, I once had a desk which I used for a dresser.) I say that I want this piece—and know that I can have it. I love this room.

In some part of the dream, a workman is busy with repairs or construction on a lower floor. He is quite happy, playing his radio as he works.

My father, but not my mother, appears in the dream. He has disposed of all my mother's collection from the other house. He has thrown away the family photographs, the diaries, the genealogical information, for which he has no use. I am sad at this, but I know it is something that cannot be changed. It must be accepted.

About seven months after this dream, both my mother and father entered a care home, and I inherited their furniture. When I moved to San Francisco into a two-story house (with a large basement), I took this furniture with me. As in the dream, the house delights me, with its marvelous nooks and spaces. The furniture fits in beautifully, and indeed the bottom of the dresser now serves as a desk. And, when I first came to see the house, a workman was doing repairs and renovation in the basement, playing his radio while he worked.

The move into a new house (a new life?) is a familiar motif in my dreams. Earlier I had a series of dreams of a "journey"—which was always wrong, a bad choice or a false move. Perhaps the house means that I should build on the self, that is, to return to the roots, incorporate, integrate, write at the desk from childhood, turn the past into its own self-reflecting fiction. Not to become a new being, a yogi, but an expanded self, one who enfolds the base identity into an enlarged personality.

A Conference on Yoga

I have just returned from a yoga conference in Colorado Springs. While there, I attended a workshop on Vedic chanting. The workshop seemed more informational than experiential. To my disappointment, we concentrated on how to sound vowel sounds and did little chanting as such.

But this morning, during meditation, I intoned certain mantras and felt a distinct vibratory sensation, especially in the throat, neck, ears, and head. It was delicate and pleasant and seemed to relax these areas, which carry considerable tension. It seems to offer a mode of access to those places (such as the nasal passages at the back of the nostrils, the place just above the palate, etc.) which are difficult or impossible to reach (relax) by other means. The sound *Om* itself is especially effective in stirring these areas.

At the conference I met a woman who had a kundalini crisis some years ago and now is doing research on others who have had this experience. She awoke in bed one night locked in an asana position, unable to move for ten minutes or so. She was hospitalized for tests, but nothing abnormal was found. She thinks her ordeal was brought on by improper *pranayama* (breathing practices), and association with a bad guru. She was written up by Dr. Lee Sanella in his book *The Kundalini Experience,* on the physical and psychological manifestations of kundalini, an area that he pioneered. She resents the fact that he merely collected the data, and offered no remedies. She herself has compiled a list of possible remedies for disturbing kundalini symptoms, such as oil on the head, and baths.

She told me that one of the yoga teachers at the conference had also had a bad kundalini experience some years ago. Although she was married, she became infatuated with one of her students. She tried to repress her feelings, but the energies came up anyway, producing numerous painful symptoms. One guru advised her that because of her condition, she would have to retire completely from the world. Instead, she went with a yoga peace group to Russia, and was ultimately cured by "toning," whatever that is.

My friend advised that persons undergoing a kundalini crisis should not attempt to work. They need to avoid *all* stress, for they have "hair-trigger responses." This certainly conforms to my experience. *(Any outer stimulus, such as a car backfiring in the distance, might send an immediate wave of pain through my body. Likewise, a delightful musical phrase might arouse instant bliss. My reactions were swifter and my senses more acute, as if I were now aware of somatic responses which before had remained below the threshold of consciousness.)* She herself seemed to be still somewhat agitated and disturbed. Apparently, she has undergone a very traumatic transformation.

Two other persons from the conference stand out in memory: a woman from Brooklyn and another from Canada. The former used to dream of a woman standing on a bluff, and was told by a seer in New York City that she had once been a Native American woman in New Mexico who used to go back and forth to Mexico to trade. She had a pet falcon that was very dear to her. This is why she is so enamored of birds in her present life.

The Canadian was formerly a hippie living in Liverpool. Now she is married and has settled down as the mother of four children. She is full of life and bounce—a thoroughly delightful person. I asked her the question that is always of such interest to me, and she said yes, she felt her own inner energies clearly. I am always hesitant to discuss this topic with anyone, since, somehow, the subject seems to be incredibly intimate, a subjective response that most people are either not aware of or are reluctant to talk about.

The conference included yogis, teachers, and many, many older women (ages fifty to seventy—I had been afraid the group would consist of mostly very young people). Two or three Tibetan priests were there—their faces seemed lifted from ancient paintings. Their features are stark, chiseled, wild; they seem as if connected to some early, lost time. This is only the second time I have seen live Tibetans.

During the conference, my head felt quite balanced, and I experienced much delightful energy, which seemed to float in the atmosphere and through me. Everything and everyone took on a sheen of beauty, but I experienced no "I am you" feelings.

A Mythical Assignment

Today, physical energy has returned, yet I feel like Jeremiah, the artist in Anne Tyler's novel, *Celestial Navigation*: "At last I have time to do all the things I wanted to do. . . . Now, what was it I wanted to do?"

In meditation this morning, I did silent *Om*s up the scale and up the spine. I felt considerable release of tension with some pleasant feelings in the lower chakras. Also, earlier in meditation, I had much pleasurable feeling in the ears as if they were relaxed and open to good energies. I seem to carry much tension in the upper chest, throat, neck, ears, and eyes. The rest of the body seems fairly relaxed.

How often the presenter or workshop leader turns to me, not as an example of serenity, but of tension. The public psychic pulls an imaginary button from my blouse, to draw out "the pain." The healer working with a group turns to me and presses his thumbs on my head. In both cases they are right. I have a headache, which they sense. P., the leader of the Rajneesh body workshop, asks about the tightness in my throat; at the yoga conference, the workshop director hurries to me and puts a sweater beneath my neck to "make me comfortable." Thus, even when I think I am relaxed and enjoying myself, I appear tense and rigid.

The woman I met in Colorado said persons with unbalanced kundalini energies should not work. So perhaps all I am fit for is to loll around, relax, discover the delight of the leaf against the sidewalk, the joy of the gentle vibration zinging the ear.

What does it mean to roll the eyeballs and feel sweet sensations (ever so quiet) in the abdomen? How do we explain a delicate evanescent pleasure (lasting barely a second) which follows the silent saying of *Om*? Probably a spiritual master would say they come from another plane—astral or subtle—but what are these realms? How do these soft sensations differ from the strong ecstasies except in intensity?

One decision I have made: I do not wish to relinquish the ordinary bodily pleasures. I do not wish to transmute the everyday physical energies into a purely spiritual emanation. I feel strongly that in order to be human, we must experience the full range of the human, even as we recollect our heavenly origins.

Sometimes, in meditation, I have the sense of riding a space vehicle that is hurtling toward Earth. Sometimes I have a sense of falling through endless cosmic space. My greatest obstacle in sustaining the meditation is my back, which hurts, always, after only a few minutes of sitting. So I move about a little, swaying the upper body, or rotating the abdomen, or thrusting the neck forward, to the left and right, like an Eastern dancer. But I have no strong images of the gods to entertain me now. My focus is on inner body sensation, which grows more and more subtle as the time passes.

So—what shall I do now? Clean my study or loll in the sun, letting the new puppy amuse me?

How do I feel at this stage of inner unfoldment? I feel as though I have been introduced to some aspect of myself of which I was previously unaware. I feel that I have integrated certain essential practices into my life in order to fill out or complete a nature otherwise incomplete. Yet I sense that much more remains concealed than the truth that has been revealed. Who we are, our origin, our destiny, our purpose, even our proper movements and direction along the path—all this is discovered gradually, as we grope clumsily in the dark, seeking familiar objects to guide us along an unknown passage.

What Have I Learned?

What is the purpose of all this? Is it a private instruction, a personal revelation to be known only by the self? Is it a means of access to a technique, a healing procedure to help others? Am I intended to share this experience, exposing my inner drama to the world? In particular, I am unwilling to admit the experiencing of raptures—something Puritan in my being balks as if feeling itself were itself a sin.

Recently, the *I Ching* cautioned me not to overlook any steps. When I asked about the beauty of the transcendent moment, which I have experienced so often, it answered: "The Clinging is the brightness in which all creatures perceive one another."

Approaching a Border

In meditation, I seem to have almost arrived at the border between sound and silence, between feeling and speech. At last I have approached the place of "self-surrender." I understand better what it would mean to give up the last final scrap of self-identity, the ultimate vestige of one's "personal" nature, to go entirely into the other, the substratum of reality—what an awesome endeavor.

This delicate energy is not, I think, the breath per se but a subtle accompaniment, a vibration awakened and sustained by the process of in/exhalation. The reality within neither desires nor experiences gratification. It is utterly self-sustaining.

Two forces propel me toward silence. One is the unwillingness to commit to work, the labor of trying to capture through verbal equivalents, the sensory (sensuous) experience. The second is the ultimate impossibility of doing so.

In Paradise, God Moves

Surely all energy disciplines—tai chi, yoga, acupuncture, acupressure, polarity therapy, internal massage, kundalini (all of which are recent discoveries for me)—are interrelated, being different aspects of the same thing. Strangely, we move about unaware of this vital flow within us. Since God (according to physics) is energy (the source of everything that is), God must be in us. When we awaken our awareness to sense this fact (which is a feeling), then we allow God to flow within us, and we are within God.

Q. What has this energy to do with ethics?
A. What has rain to do with justice?

The Task of Women

The continuing task of woman is to heal the many divisions, to link right and left brains (rational and intuitive functions); join spirit with physical being; and to fulfill both domestic and public roles. In order for these splits to be mended, society must revise its age-old notions of what is "acceptable," what is "unacceptable" behavior for women, and relinquish the labels used for centuries to force women into patterns of approved behavior. To attain psychological wholeness, the being must incorporate the Shadow (acknowledge the unknown aspects) into the whole self. Because woman has been deprived of this opportunity, much of her essential nature has been forced into the subconscious realm, where it calls for recognition and rescue. It is indeed a significant moment in history when an entire sex rises and demands the right to integrate the self.

Words and Energy

Those who know, do not speak—because description is impossible. We can say, "The sensation is unimaginably subtle." Or we can say, "I feel it here, I feel it there—it moves, sometimes like a flash, more often like a slow remembrance of a place neglected or forgotten or not yet awakened in awareness." We can say, "This is energy, freeing and opening and making pleasurable various areas of the body. This is a restoration of the body to its natural state." We can say, "The feeling seems to ride the breath, coming and going in bliss with its ever so subtle rise and fall. Yet it is not the breathing per se. The feeling is *aroused* by breath, like a delicate manipulation of the inner being."

Exercises I Have Discovered for Experiencing the Energies

Lie flat on your back and slowly relax, feeling whatever sensations are present in your body. With regular, yogic breathing (fill your lungs from the bottom up), turn your head as slowly as possible from right to left, back, then left to right. Pause frequently, noting the various feelings in your body.

After face and eye massages, rotate your eyes left, right, up, and down, then revolve them backwards in your head (in imagination, of course—but try, anyway.) Then move them in micromovements just a bit. Feel the energies in your abdomen. Then imagine the movement (without moving) and see what you feel.

Intone *Om* silently. Note the vibrations in your head, throat, chest, or stomach. Note the energy flows that are aroused.

Move your jaws slightly back and forth, up and down, to release tension about the ears.

The exquisite feelings produced by such exercises seem to proceed from some level more subtle than that of hatha yoga. Indeed, the *asanas* (as I know them) seem quite gross (unsubtle) compared to this activity, which is mainly breath, micromovements, and concentration.

But how can I sustain this mood? Even writing this, I feel tension rising in my neck and eyes, prickles beginning. Now not only reading, but writing is difficult—any use of the eyes causes tension and pain, though I can see (focus) clearly with them.

Yes—much tension, pain arose. I alleviated it some with more massage and pressure on ball of foot, neck, lower back, and other places. But—why the tension? Why the releases? Should I do no reading or writing at all? Or is it an aftereffect of the pleasure of meditation? Or do I meditate wrong? Or too long? Or too subtly?

Massage and Inner Feelings

On Saturday, I attended an all-day workshop on massage. When Joanne worked on my head and face, I felt extremely delicate, sensuous energies flow through my temples and inside my skull. The feeling is midway between a mystical experience and sex, which are, of course, profoundly related.

Then, on the day after the workshop, I became acutely aware of certain deep feelings (sorrow and grief, particularly) when I thought of my mother, and her condition, and of Kate, and our relationship. All my emotions, including those I keep carefully buried deep within, seemed to rise to the surface, particularly those relating to the sadness of love and the passage of time. Clearly, the experience of the workshop had brought these responses out.

The Neuro-Electrical Basis of All Feeling

In recent weeks, my meditations have grown more and more subtle, moving from definite sensation to tenuous, borderline response. This morning I felt—or almost felt—a gentle release within, as soft as if the cheeks were stroked lightly with a rose. It is as if I have gone from being overwhelmed by ecstasy into ever less pronounced, more refined levels. As the intensity of impulse has diminished, my capacity for detecting nuance has increased; the whole thing has played like a game of hide and seek, with the initial signals so strong I could not fail to notice them. Once my attention was captured, the impulses became progressively less and less intense, until now, even their existence is not absolutely certain. It is like, say, a melody played at first quite loudly, then at lower and lower volume, until at last I am uncertain whether I am hearing an external melody, or listening to an inner music. I think I am now approaching—or am at—a threshold, the border between sensation and thought.

I feel as though I am being exposed to the neuro-electrical basis of all human feeling and activity—the impulses that under-lie and potentiate all affect, movement, thought, desire, and doing. Without this network of energy, the constant exchange of impulses traveling to and from the myriad points of the neural (muscular?) system, no sensation could occur and no response take place. This observation says nothing new. But the *experiencing* of this level of activity is to me extremely new.

Experimenting with Love

Recently, I have been experimenting with love. I allow myself more and more to *feel* and *see* the love I have for others. I am struck with wonder at their beauty. I truly see them with a lover's eye, though they can be anyone at all—a new acquaintance, an ordinary person I pass on the sidewalk, an old friend. Surely this is *caritas,* the love of the heart that is all-accepting in its embrace. I've had—and noted—similar experiences in the past, but they are becoming more frequent, sometimes lasting for days.

Last week I discovered two other people who have had this experience. Carol says she has often entered this state and that for her, it is sometimes accompanied by a sensation of feeling ill. She agrees with me that some chemical must actually be released in the system, triggering both responses. Carol says that she is certain her grandmother also experienced these mystical flashes—you could see her face light up in recognition at such moments.

One student, E., has had similar experiences, but she is somewhat frightened of them, as they recall for her a time of schizophrenic breakdown. I understand why she might feel anxiety, but with time one can get used to anything.

Yesterday, when I took this manuscript to L.'s house, it came to me that I must now prepare for the second, completing half of the experience of love. I must let the love that others have for me come through. I must realize it, not on the intellectual level, but on the felt plane of experience.

How strange if what began as wildness of spirit ends as "Christian" love of all being.

On Love: What We Fear

What we fear is that the new state, the altered way of seeing, is, somehow, an aberration, product of a disturbed psyche. Perhaps one is trapped by illusion, illusion bred of the private self or reinforced by the social collective. Yet the fact remains, these are new ways of seeing on the literal level, there are periods—days, weeks even—of raw beauty. That is, faces are "unmasked," illuminated, shining as from an inner source. *All* creatures take a turn toward the angelic, which is to say, they become spirits tinged with mystery, yet still expressing their inherent individuality. They have *personality,* particular psychological definition. We can clearly distinguish one being from another. As persons, they are perhaps nothing extraordinary. But somehow, the inner radiance of self, freed of its petty concerns and limitations, comes forth, and is beautiful in its literal, physical manifestation. One looks and is awed, and loves with admiration, with a love experienced as wonder, without need or desire. To behold is sufficient. How could one describe what one sees? The moment is its own definition.

This love, which asks nothing for itself, realizes in humility that what it has previously known is without substance, what it has called its ideas a void, what it has termed its wisdom a fallacy. Thus stripped of all prior assumptions, it can only accept that which is given—the vision of love which must be God.

Then a Break Occurs

And then—a break, a tear, a rupture. Something happens, the spirit withdraws, the inner eye closes, the self proclaims its own insufficiency. Faces are once more only faces, one feels disturbed, the body tenses, the nerves begin to moan. There are the prickling sensations roaming at random over the flesh, there is a tense shudder within. The head throbs, one undergoes spiritual collapse. What has failed? What law is broken, which principle violated? Always, failure to meet the human situation appropriately—emotions of disgust, anger even, at another's disturbing attitudes or action, or a sense of self-rejection and inadequacy. The personal system *closes*—on physical and spiritual levels, there is an agonized fall into the limited self.

Then once more, for many days, I experienced love as an altered state, and recognized, with a shock, my oneness with others, sometimes thinking, this is my own face I look upon, this other is myself, I am this being.

Listening to Music

You have been tuned
for this moment
for a thousand years.
Each star at midnight,
each drop from the well
became who you are,
this vessel of anguished rapture,
flesh, muscle, bone.

Once there was a divine pulsation in heaven.
You and all that is
are its unfoldment,
summoning the world to being.

Listen.
Your blood knows how to be with
this dark intensity,
this opened vein of love,
like a flowing stillness before a storm,
a river moving quietly
through a hurricane.

It is beginning once more.

Part 4

Walking in the Two Worlds

This Music of Light

Imagine a Buddha
with light around
her head.
Her ear, the one
you are sleeping in.
Her breath,
the rhythm of your sleep,
your body her sounding board.

You are the one she has come for.
Now is your moment of honey and fire.

You sit in the midst
of your silence.
The world tide recedes,
taking even your name.
You cry out as the light
enters your heart.

It Has Begun Again

It has begun again. After weeks, months, even, of absence, *it,* the feeling, the sensation, has returned. Night before last, as I sat in the evening seeking merely to relax, it came, this time not as a wild, overwhelming torrent, but rather in extremely pleasant impulses that touched here and there, including a little in the back of the head. Today it came stronger and continued during Chi Gong exercises till sides, feet, cheeks were "turned on." It was delicious, but not an engulfing rapture. Yet I know it was there. Only once in recent months has this occurred, after the language conference. Then I had a good yoga session, possibly from the energies of those I had been with during that time.

Night before last, I started rereading Thompson's *The Time Falling Bodies Take to Light,* the book that played such a prominent role in my original kundalini experience. Once more, this book seemed to prompt a mysterious awakening of energies within. As if these words touched sacred centers, as if the syllables themselves were charges of energy. The sacred is then experienced as the realm of sweet sensation. Such words as *yoga, Tibetan, kundalini* act as secret springs, to release an ancient response.

Dreams of My Father

My father died July 20. Here are some dreams surrounding this event:

On July 5, I left (with Kate) for a vacation in Yellowstone and Jackson Hole, Wyoming. One or two days before I left, my friend Carol called me in midafternoon, awakening me from a nap on the couch. The phone call interrupted a dream, which I immediately told her. In the dream, "someone" was trying to burn Carol's house down while she was gone. I was very concerned, and felt I should get word to her. Then the dream switched. Now

I was driving by our old family home, the house where I grew up (a red brick bungalow on a small lot). They were "closing the house up" by placing wide boards (vertical, like a fence) all around it, like a box or a tomb.

Clearly, I associated myself with Carol in the dream. Her father died only seven months ago from Alzheimer's, something few people knew much about at the time. His last years were a great ordeal for all in her family. Now her mother is having some problems, having to do with investing the money he left. If she loses it, she will have little income for her own later years. Carol's "house" (her family) is indeed threatened, as is mine.

Then, on July 20, my father died suddenly of a heart attack (he was ninety-one); he toppled like a tree in the forest. My mother witnessed his fall. The emergency crew were unable to revive him.

I saw him twice at the funeral home. The first time, before he was "cosmeticized," he looked natural. For a moment, I had a clear glimpse of his strong features—he looks like a Roman senator, I thought. Indeed, he was, to me, beautiful. Yet, one could also discern an expression of pain, possibly the pain of his last moments. It was as if I observed on his features nobility alternating with pain. Both were present.

I found the last book he had read, only a few weeks before: it was Gandhi's autobiography. In the margin, he had written: "God is Truth," which was, I felt, a highly appropriate conclusion to the life of an avowed atheist. He was buried in the little family plot in the local cemetery. I stayed with my mother in the care home for several days afterward, to help her with the transition to widowhood. I was acutely aware of the loving attitudes there, and, once again, had the sense of the inner beauty of everyone I met.

Childhood Revisited

I have spent quite a lot of time with my mother recently. One day, while I was visiting, I went for a walk through my old neighborhood past our onetime house and on down a couple of blocks near what was formerly a pasture with ponds. Our old house is now quite shabby and run-down, and children's toys are scattered about. The Chinese elms my father planted fifty years ago have been cut to the stump. The pasture has been turned into a small city park with playground equipment. The ponds have been drained. How terrifying it is to witness the physical changes brought by time (as if part of one's personal past has been obliterated).

When I was a child, we (the Greggs and I) made our forays into Jamieson's land (he owned the dairy on the hill) like ritual journeys into sacred space. First we went through the barbed wire fence bordering Clegern Road, pulling it apart in a certain place to get through. Then we passed by the old muddy ponds, which were good for little but catching crawdads (a pastime I had no interest in). At the far diagonal of the field, we slipped through yet another wire fence, and made our way to the pigsty, which smelled to heaven of hogs and mud. After observing and exclaiming on these untidy creatures, we went on to the "brambles." These were long cylinders of brush into which we could climb and roll about, giggling and shouting as we romped. Finally, we arrived at our ultimate destination—"the rock."

The rock was a ledge overhanging the terminus of a dry creek bed. At some time in the past, the creek had hollowed out a cavity below, not a real cave, but enough of an indentation to stir our imaginations. The rock was to us somehow mysterious, magic even. It seemed connected to some distant past whose history we could not know. It suggested real caves, mountains, boulders, rushing streams of which we had very few in our neighborhood.

Sometimes we went even farther, crossing the county road into the next field. The red clay road was banked by a slender wall of dirt that had built up through the years between the roadbed and the ditch. Somehow, this wall also hinted of mystery. What was it? How had it come to be there? You could put your ear to the poles along the roadside (for telephone lines, I assume) and hear a thrilling hum, as if they were charged with the energy of the universe, as if you were monitoring secret messages from unknown sources. Sometimes we went farther still into yet another field, with its unknown woods and canyons. Always, in these regions, I felt in touch with something profound, something quite marvelous and unspoken. Looking back, I would call these excursions experiences of mystical union with nature. I think all children possess this capacity for transcendence, until it is driven out of them by life.

Today these areas are given over to housing developments catering to the affluent. Ponds, pigpen, brambles—they're all gone, as if we had never made our sacred journeys. From the road, you can still see the rock, now backing an apartment complex. I suppose the developers couldn't think of a way to get rid of it, so had to build around it. A shopping center stands nearby, and the houses and their circle drives.

The Mask of Silenus Explained

Earlier I wrote of MKBL, as he first introduced himself, who was our spirit communicator (Master of the Kabbalah) on the Ouija board, and who became a dramatic influence in other ways as well. We began the connection in January or February, and by the summer, when we left for Boulder, my creative imagination was richly stirred. I wrote poems of the hero's journey and of the Great Mother (both important symbols awakening in consciousness). I studied the Hebrew alphabet, and in other ways followed MKBL's direction, preparing for initiation into the Golden Dawn, on the inner planes.

On the day of my "initiation" into this presumed occult realm, I had gazed in the mirror, and been startled by what I saw there—a face that was grossly sensual, animalistic, as if it sprang from the deep core of some ancient Earth-principle of carnality or lust.

> Behold the mask of Silenus
> gross mirror mocker
> of the Dionysian school,
> your father and your guide.

I am unsure how I identified the mask as Silenus—why I called it "father" and "guide." I was not certain what a "mask of Silenus" was. I looked up Silenus, and found that he was the teacher of Dionysus, god of ecstasy. I named the symbol, and wrote the poem, but on another level I rejected it as an aspect of self.

A few days ago, I was reading some comments by Jung on the kundalini phenomenon, and felt sweet energies stir, mainly in the first and second chakras. A short time later, I discovered an essay by C. Kerényi, "Man and Mask," in *Spiritual Disciplines* (papers from the Eranos Yearbooks). In this article, he discusses the role of the Silenus mask in ancient initiation rites for boys entering manhood.

The first example is a mural in the Villa dei Misteri in Pompeii where Silenus, accompanied by two boy satyrs, appears to the right of Dionysus and Ariadne. One satyr peers into a silver bowl. In it he sees the reflection, not of his own face, but of a Silenus mask: "The boy thinks that he sees himself, and he recognizes himself as one of the older men, fathers and teachers, who had dominated and led him up to now and to whose number he now belongs. It is a uniting transformation, accomplished by the mask as image of the father: *Sileni patris imago*. The boy is united with the fathers and is initiated as a procreating man."

A second mural at Pompeii depicts a similar scene, which Kerényi interprets as "the initiation of the [boy Satyrs] into the mystery that they, as male beings, are identical with Father Silenus." Kerényi thinks the mask was also used in Rome as well as at the Athenian festival of Apatheria, in which boys were initiated into maturity.

Sometimes the depictions show a butterfly (emblem of rebirth) issuing from the mouth of the mask. Kerényi further comments, "[T]he meeting of man himself with the non-individual—whether divine or animal, heroic or even typical—human face . . . is an overwhelming encounter, whether it takes place in the secret cult or in the theater. How—the psychologist will say—can an encounter with the archetype, in the case of the

Silenus mask, assuredly a father archetype, fail to be profoundly moving."

Surely, the mask and the discovery of its meaning (the latter coming so close upon my father's death) has to do with the operation of the father (masculine) principle in my own life. During the episode that led up to the revelation of the mask in the mirror, my "guide" was male; though he was a spirit, I felt a strong connection.

At the time of this earlier experience, which produced such psychic shock and spiritual dismay, I renounced the entire project (inner psychic awakening) in which I was engaged. But ultimately, almost secretly, I was preparing (or being prepared) to "come in" through another door, which proved to be, like the first, initiation through the body/spirit. The first involved the evocation of the animus in the guise of the poet-spirit guide, the fiery creative impulse. But I could not deal with the image in the mirror as a reflection of self. Later on, kundalini arose through a deep integration of male and female elements (Shiva and Shakti in union being the dominant symbol). For me, this image of male-female united emerged as a sacred archetype exposing and confirming the union of human and divine, with the creative, sexual energies swept up into and united with spiritual essence.

Jung has pointed out that in the East, the unconscious is located above, but with us (the West), it is below. I think a more accurate perception would be that the conscious is contained in and surrounded by the unconscious. Hence it (the unconsciousness) is both "above" and "below"—and both are areas we have blotted from awareness. Perhaps the "below" of the West is peopled with those gods we have transformed to demons. The East, in Tantra, permits these gods (divine energies) full play, looking toward the liberation (in the mind) as transcendence. The West presses the libido into the id where they (the sacred images) turn to wrathful demons (repression, anxiety, etc.). Freud sought to restore these divine "impulses" to the conscious level, but he denied their heavenly connection, reducing them to the "merely human." The East elevates them to the highest levels. In Tantra, by joining the gods, we become divine.

The Opening of the Heart Chakra

Three or four years ago, at the beginning of this kundalini adventure, my friend the therapist said, "The opening of the heart chakra is the deepest ecstasy of all." At the time, I had not consciously experienced this opening, and could only wonder what bliss could surpass that which I had already felt. What she said is true. When the heart opens, the chest is flooded with rapture, at once so delicate and so intense, it can scarcely be borne. One moans, as if in the toils of love.

Where does such rapture come from? Last week, I left school early both Wednesday and Thursday afternoons, and "gathered energy." On Thursday afternoon, I had exercised (through chi gong movements), danced to music, and gone to my "yoga area" to continue my meditation. I sat cross-legged, listening to music playing on the radio. I moved my shoulders and chest slowly to the music and was quickly flooded with intense and incredibly sweet sensation in the heart and chest area. Thus it was that my heart "opened" at last. It was, indeed, the "sweetest ecstasy of all."

How can this be?

Male and Female Joined

Two nights ago, I dreamed that I had grown a second head. It was myself, but male, complete with mustache. The male was joined to the female (also me) at the back of the neck—like the Roman two-headed god, Janus. The male "twin" was not as fully developed as the female, but it was definitely part of my identity. I wondered what I should do about this "problem"; should I have the head removed in an operation, like an extra appendage? I decided to keep myself as I was. People were amazed at my appearance, but then, this gave me a special distinction.

Clearly, this dream refers to the ongoing process of integration of male and female components within the self, and relates to the recent episodes involving my father and Silenus.

A New Setting, A Familiar Pattern

During the ensuing years, I ascended and descended the ladder of love many times, in ecstasy and despair. The previous pattern continued: sometimes I was convinced I had at last achieved inner balance. At other times, I suffered psychological and/or physical pain such that I was certain I was headed toward utter destruction.

After I retired from teaching, Kate and I had moved to San Francisco, where I hoped that in this more progressive environment I would find experts who could help me interpret my experience, which I felt, finally, ready to share. For the most part, I was disappointed. One, a university teacher of ancient chakra philosophy, never returned or commented on the manuscript I so hesitantly offered. Another, a therapist who had done special research in the area of kundalini awakening, seemed only slightly interested in my account. Still others, students of various metaphysical paths, did not understand the nature of the story I was attempting to tell, dismissing it as merely "personal processing." When I asked an expert teacher of Taoist practice about my feelings of "ecstasy" during yoga practice, I was told that the ancient texts mentioned only energies that felt "cold, hot, or like electricity."

How ironic, I thought, that I finally felt sufficient confidence to reveal my experience, only to discover an almost total lack of interest on the part of others. Nonetheless, I held to my inner conviction that what I had encountered was part of a wider, possibly universal, expansion of consciousness, now occurring on the planet, manifesting in various ways. And I hoped that someday soon, as more and more persons experienced this overwhelming transformation, there would be an increasing awareness of its implications, and more support networks for those involved.

As the culmination of a course of therapy with a lesbian feminist in San Francisco, I experienced a period of openness during which I saw several inner faces, and felt many deep emotions I had hidden for so long. (These inner revelations were in fact triggered first by a body worker, whose very first touch—when she lay hands on my back—evoked a flood of feelings and emotions, and started the train of inner imagery.)

During this period (which lasted several weeks), I re-experienced in full my childhood anger at being held, repressed, and controlled. I confronted the devastation wrought upon the helpless child when the parent prevents her from feeling, much less expressing, the basic, normal emotions of the human condition. I worked through these, releasing them one after another as impulses of intense anger, desire, and spiritual exaltation.

Even though I had progressed to some of the peaks in spiritual experience, it was now necessary to go back and take care of unfinished business on the personal level. First, we are whisked to the top of the mountain. But after we admire the view, we find ourselves once again at the bottom. We must ascend again, this time on hands and knees.

I saw many internal images (during this time) of those who might be my spiritual teachers, or else symbols of motifs that would appear soon in my life in one way or another. These images included a handsome, bearded, high-collared Middle Easterner (possibly Jewish), who seemed to be intellectual—someone who hung out a lot in libraries and museums; a Native American medicine man; a Mithraic priest; and a rather plain and uninteresting young Chinese woman (merchant class). Soon thereafter, I attended a workshop on shamanic practice, and heard a lecture on astrology based on early Mithraic perspectives. And the young Chinese woman became my pupil, whom I tutored in English.

Mongolian Overtone Chanting

Sometimes, when spiritual pilgrims begin their journeys, they travel about the world, seeking masters and teachers to aid them. I took no such geographic voyage, but when I moved to San Francisco, I encountered many such "remarkable women and men," who either lived in the area or visited from time to time. Each contributed something significant to my growth, but none served as an external guru.

On Saturday and Sunday, I attended a workshop given by Jill Purce on sound with special emphasis on Mongolian Overtone Chanting. When I first heard the overtones (in the group), the rapture penetrated my heart. The sound Jill made, as well as that of the class chanting with her, is wondrous, something not of this world. Obviously sacred, ritualistic, a connection to the other world. The overtones are sometimes called "ghost music." Jill says strange and miraculous things can happen to those who chant.

This week, with time given to practice, to rapture, has been better than all of the previous summer with its journeys here and there, its multiple-surface encounters, its immersion in secular writing and ordinary adventure. What is this journey I am making into the self?

Today I had an image in meditation. (It is unusual for me to "see" anything internally these days.) It was of a boy about thirteen or fourteen in a peaked Tibetan hat, holding sacred implements in his hand. He had delicate lips and features; he was someone chosen for high (spiritual) position. I felt it was I in some other life. Who? What is this connection? What am I to do in this incarnation?

As I sit here, I feel stinging and burning, all over—is it blocked kundalini, or allergies, or both, the one producing blockage of the other? Should I vacuum and risk extreme headache? Or wait it out, and perhaps increase my misery by the hour?

Lights in the Head, and a Workshop in Chi Gong

After the second day of the chanting workshop, I twice awoke in the middle of the night with a sense of brilliant light penetrating my brain—something like my dream a while back after I visited the Rosicrucian center in San Jose, when I had a sense of beings scanning my head with brilliant lights to know who I was.

The "ecstatic meditation" I referred to continued again on Thursday and Friday. On Saturday and Sunday I attended another workshop—that of Khaleghl Quinn, on "Reclaim Your Power," a mixture of philosophy and flowing chi gong practice.

She herself was the flower of the summer, the commanding being who silences and awes simply by her forceful presence. She began life in El Paso, Texas, a mixture of black and Cherokee, with a little Tibetan thrown in, she says. She is tall, imposing, full-bodied, radiating the strength of the ancient goddesses. She is composed, thoroughly poised at all times. She has a beautiful voice. When she does chi gong, she becomes something other, a hypnotic blend of grace and sensuous movement. To imitate her gestures from the student's position is to partake of her sensuous energies. At the end, she and Vicki dello Joio, my regular teacher, did a "dance" that contained limited footwork, but in which arms and hands moved in delicate grace. These subtle movements stirred delicious inner energies, each minute turning producing a corresponding sweet impulse within myself as watcher. I felt as though I had moved back many centuries in time and witnessed an ancient, sacred performance, one as beloved then as now. Their movements were intoxicating, as if one were in the presence of an irresistible lover.

During the workshop, we did a simple relaxation exercise with partners. My partner was, as is so often the case, probably the last person in the room I would have sought out. She was a very trim, foxy young woman in shorts, with curly long blond hair, someone who seemed far apart from me in age and appearance. But she invited me to join her and gave me a deeply relaxing experience. I had been squeezing in various body regions before, as if I was about to get a headache, but she cured me in short order.

When we changed places and I put my hand on her forehead and skull, the temperature of both of us shot up. She said, "You have lots of chi." As I continued, we both began to flush and perspire. The experience for me was "energy as heat." When we finished, she chose to lie still for quite some time. Later, I asked her if the experience was okay, and she said she had "blissed out." This was very encouraging for me. I would like to be able to give others this experience through energy work.

Losing Interest in the World

This has been a very busy weekend—I did no practice Friday, Saturday, or Sunday, but I did a lot otherwise. I saw the intensely disturbing movie *Robin Hood:* an unfolding sequence of blood and gore (very distressing). I attended a concert of ancient Japanese music played on similarly ancient instruments, and a poetry reading with Adrienne Rich, Sharon Olds, and Galway Kinnell. I also had dim sum with Kate and a new student from China, but nothing—not the music, poetry, or the stimulating student from a foreign country—begins to compare in terms of pleasure (pure sensuous enjoyment) with my daily practice. Does this mean I must turn from art, music, intellect, multicultural encounters into the realm of pure feeling? Will I care nothing for the world and its pursuits? Will I withdraw into a knot of subjective bliss?

Or is (as I had supposed) the ecstasy a mode of being I am here to help deliver to others to help us all reconnect with our source? Am I burning up (exorcising) my interest in certain related areas in order to focus more specifically on the central mission? Who knows?

Well, I am stubborn enough, and solitary enough, to continue on this (unchosen) course. I have a sense of correctness (this is what I should be doing), but little of ultimate purpose or grand design. Meanwhile, I'm here, doing my practice and sighing with pleasure.

On Enlightenment

One of the great errors of the spiritual path is to assume there is a goal, an ultimate state to be reached, a final "enlightenment." For most of us (the few highest beings such as Buddha being exceptions) enlightenment or final realization does not take place—nor should it.

If we were "enlightened"—completely filled with presence, light—we would immerse ourselves continuously in our bliss, letting it waft through us perpetually until we were pure fields of rapture. To experience this, we would need to take leave of this world and exist as mere clouds of joy.

To do what is needed at this time, we must retain our contact with the world of practical reality. We must live in the world, experience its involvements, its drama, its fluctuations of pain alternating with pleasure, in order that we may together move forward in our common progress.

The gurus and swamis who promise enlightenment as a permanent state to be achieved do us a disservice. The aim is to move constantly forward, progressing as our nature permits, in cooperation with universal forces, neither hurrying nor dallying on the path. "The path is the goal." Indeed.

Homosexuality and Kundalini

Both homosexuality and kundalini are mysteries, and those who experience them discover that they display many common features: no one knows the cause or source of either. Both, because they are so little understood, are feared, and sometimes denounced as profane. Both control the life from within, being neither chosen nor not chosen. (Does one choose to be alive, to breathe?) Both are sources of the deepest creativity, of joy and pain; to repress either is to stifle the essential life force of the being. Both (in their highest expression) combine the spiritual and physical, or rather, both insist that these two realms are in fact the same.

Each can be viewed as a mirror reflection of the other; they are like different manifestations of a single impulse. Both underline our connection to a higher source that we can feel but never know, a power not explicable in ordinary terms, but whose expression is all around us and in us. And both are sources of extreme power, to be approached with respect and reverence. To abuse either is to incur grave personal consequences.

Fear of Nonexistence

In San Francisco, Kate quickly found new friends and interests through her job. I, on the other hand, initially seemed to lose all sense of my identity (I had been a university teacher for most of my adult life), and for years struggled to find a new self. Alone, I did my practice. Alone, I went through my various trials and inner triumphs. She seemed uninterested in the journey I had embarked on, and turned to other pursuits as her life opened to new avenues. Fortunately, I soon discovered Rumi, and he provided much solace for me in my isolated state. I was for the first time living in a city, where traffic rushed by my front window and sirens echoed throughout the day. I saw misery on the street, and suffering in doorways. I knew that somewhere in this maelstrom were kindred souls and congenial activities, but I was at first overwhelmed by the plethora of choices. Gradually, I came to terms with my new setting, and found kindred souls with whom to share experiences.

Kate and I had continued to live together all these years, but now simply as friends and housemates. I had encouraged her to find another sexual partner, and so she was embarking on a new relationship. To my dismay, the prospect of this change aroused deep fear and anxiety on my part. Obviously, I was grappling with ancient childhood issues, and these had to be cleared before I could experience major spiritual growth. Finally, I wrote about my inner struggle in my notebook, letting my thoughts come up without control, the impulse taking me where it would. I wrote without concern for style or shape, simply expressing my intense feelings and speculating on the implications of suffering for incarnation. In effect, I had to go back, to deal with the challenges of one level before I could proceed to those of the next. Here is a sample of my writing at this time:

What am I afraid of?

- I am afraid I do not exist.

- I am afraid to exist.

- I am something that is a lot of trouble.

All of this, clearly, relates to the early mother relationship. The rupture of the bond, and the interminable effort to repair it. The child, wounded, depleted, damaged. The child, afraid, insecure, filled with anxiety and apprehension. The child sent out, carrying its inner sense of insufficiency into a threatening world. The child, defeated, chagrinned. Retreating into the world of make-believe (the books), nature (which accepts and condones and does not judge), the animal friend.

All of life is a search for the lost friend/lover, the mother who will accept, support, and nourish. Who will sanction not only the inner self but the body and its uses. Who will allow the child to experience the joy of selfhood, without condemnation or censure.

Sometimes I think what happened (the awakening of kundalini) was indeed a call to Buddhahood, the primordial transformation of flesh to spirit. Sometimes I believe the event prompted a leap into a prior incarnation, in this case, as a larger, wiser being with capacities far beyond my own. Again, I wonder if what is recollected is simply the bliss of the womb-state, before a sense of self-identity forms, and our nascent consciousness knows only the life-spirit that is quickening it, moving it toward the human level. In any event, what is remembered is a prior state, a time of blissful being, of wholeness and perfection, before the spirit was torn and divested. What remains (after birth and early childhood) is a partial self, a creature programmed to see itself as woefully imperfect, disastrously incomplete.

Is this a universal fate? Does everyone experience the agony of the mutilated spirit? Or is it only certain ones, children undermined and enfeebled before the journey has yet begun? If we are fragments drifted to Earth, from a larger, more complete being, what is the point of this diminution? Perhaps the prior self, knowing only its own strength and completion, can discover the nature of weakness only through incarnation as a lesser soul, thereby experiencing what it is to be blocked and frustrated.

The Original Terror

I am trying to return. I am trying to go back, to experience the original terror. Was it womb-fear, a time when I knew that I faced imminent annihilation (when my mother almost had me aborted)? Was it the deep sense of betrayal, that the one who loved me, who had "called me into being," was prepared to destroy me, to blot out my awareness even before it fully *was?*

Such soul sickness, such fear. Such dread as reverberated through the system. I was nothing but this—a ball of fear, a knot of anguish. I was saved through divine intervention. Something "stayed her hand." She did not prepare. She canceled the appointment. I was allowed to be born.

What, then, remained? We were locked, both of us, in a union violated at its inception. We were both called on to act out roles in a deceptive relationship: she pretending love for an offspring whom she essentially rejected. I, hoping against hope, struggling to find acceptance when at another level came constant confirmation of the deepest fear.

So where is my place? How do I fit into this alien world? I who had already been judged and found wanting? What was implanted in me, at every second, at each turning, was the deep sense of unworthiness, of insufficiency, of not being adequate, so I drifted into ever deeper layers of soul sickness, anxiety, and denial.

Somewhere at the bottom of the bog resided the monster ready to raise his head. Ready to bellow the truth, the horrible, unthinkable conviction: she doesn't love you. You are an imposition, something in the way.

There is no solution, only a retreat, into books, daydreams, fantasies. To ease the threat, to assuage the fear, to provide temporary respite.

It is one of the most familiar dramas in human experience. Rejection by the mother. How simple. How prevalent. How devastating. And it waits, always, an unseen trap, ready to spring and clutch where we least expect. A drama waiting to repeat in similar circumstances. This is the fundamental scenario, the repeated scene, the reiterated question: How can I exist if she does not love me? Who can I be if I am no one in her eyes?

We go along, we muddle through, we have our minor successes (but never allow ourselves to feel them). We score our relative triumphs. Lovers come and tell us everything is okay. In the beloved's arms we relax and find—a moment, a year, years of solace. We are healed. We think that now, at last, the wound is healed, finally we are whole. We feel energy, spirit, confidence, we become a "whole person." We act without impairment, as a total, not a partial, self. Then the lover leaves. And we are, again, thrown into the pit, the place of disconsolate darkness where, once more, we are confirmed in our nonbeing. Can anything erase this dread? Can any act of preparedness, caution, forestall the recurrent death of spirit? It is like the Christ-drama: death and resurrection constantly reenacted. Finally we pull out, we go up, we emerge. But, in order to "arise," we must first be annihilated, explode into nothing once again.

What causes her (the mother) to act this way? She herself has been exposed to great spiritual abuse. She learned, early on, that she was a burden, an intrusion, an unwelcome presence. She was threatened, shamed, violated at the core. She never knew acceptance and love. Rejected, she became rejecting—of the daughter who reflected her self, the female, the miniature replica of her own being. Like a child who enacts an adult drama on her doll, she projected her own misery and sense of insufficiency onto you, the child. She is not culpable—but O, the dreadful consequences.

She sought, above all else, a studied and carefully maintained appearance as a defense against the judgment of the world. In addition, she inculcated in the child the fear of feeling on all levels. She presented the body as a place of shame, and it and all its responses, even of joy, happiness, delight, were to be squelched and suppressed for they were not appropriate to the human condition. So that the child (I) could experience little more than anxiety, little else than dread. I operated from a basic assumption that I was not as adequate as the others, that I didn't measure up, didn't meet expectations. How can you experience self-worth if you know you are damaged goods?

Advice from Within

Once more, I sought the advice of the teacher within.

Q. *Are we nothing but this? The mother complex, with all its attendant fears, anxieties?*

A. Obviously not. Obviously there are many productive realms within and outside the sphere of the complex. More is involved. Is a handicapped person only the handicap?

Q. *What is the relation of the mother complex to the discovery of the self?*

A. You chose it to drive you to a crucial moment of ego annihilation. It became a tool to propel you to a new level of being. It was the fundamental script on which all later romantic dramas were founded. Through the painful reenactment of the first loss, ultimately a way to recover the original self (at least in part) was found. If you had not suffered so internally, you might have remained in a state of happy apathy. Mud turtles in the Sun versus panthers taking chances. You risked a great deal, and won something precious through your suffering.

Q. *What now?*

A. Since you here uncover the deep basis of your feeling, you are better prepared to cope with it. Adjust your self-image accordingly. Don't cater to self-pity. Acknowledge the tragic consequences of the past. Move on to a more highly integrated level.

You know this truth, even in your bones, and this knowledge will arm you against further assault.

Focus on what is most important in your life. If symptoms or feelings arise, speak to them—say, yes, old acquaintance, I feel your familiar presence. I know your source, and hence have no need to admit you or give you permanent residence. Be active—say, "Begone!" and they will disappear. Find ways to affirm the self. You have a gift to deliver—not least of all, to your self.

Facing the Monster

This event (the psychological trauma of loss) has rushed to its conclusion or at least achieved a partial resolution. How quickly I have passed from despair to happiness.

This time I resolved not to jump to the other, higher level. This time, I vowed to face the specter on its own ground, to stand firm, to deal with "it" in the realm of the "real," the familiar world of all our days. And astonishingly, I saw for the first time ever how the two dramas played simultaneously, one shaping and reinforcing the other. The old mother script—how eager to activate, how quick to take over and control the current scenario. In the past when the crisis (of betrayal, of loss) occurred, I was always in a state of deep attachment to a love object, idealized out of all relation to reality. Onto her I had projected all the warmth, love, nurturance, and acceptance denied me by the mother. Thus, when she left, it was as if my own mother had betrayed me.

Earlier, when the scene repeated, I abandoned self and its claims (ego-death), and kundalini rushed in to take the place of the human lover. This time, the scene was different. I realized in the midst of my agony that in fact, I was not being unjustly deprived of a love object, that I had, in fact, suggested and sought this very end (for the other to find a new lover), that I was being freed—from responsibilities for another's happiness, expectations of all kinds I could not meet. That I had friends, interests sufficient to provide other activities independent of her.

So I took my own advice. I spoke directly to the feelings of inner worthlessness, self-rejection. I vowed not to succumb. I took control of events, not letting the feeling master me. And the ghost was dispelled. The monster lost its steam. The complex was resolved, as if in a Freudian case history. I got to the bottom of it (went to the bottom of despair). I saw by feeling again the old emotions, recognizing them for what they were, the leftover remains of childhood trauma, ancient attachments betrayed, infantile terrors reenacted.

Since then, for a week or so, I have lived a life without anxiety or fear; and I do it alone with the self, not depending on or seeking an outside support (lover), needing no one to confirm either my existence or self-worth. Although I did not seek kundalini ecstasy as part of the experience, my energies have begun to flow in sweet, soft vibrations flowing in gentle delight throughout the body. I have found the right teacher for this movement-energy arousing process. I have told her my story (the sudden eruption of kundalini) and she understood my words, one of the few ever to do so.

I feel great relief, and inner release. My energy has come up. I am experiencing the city without depression for the first time since I moved here four years ago. I am cured! (I know this is a dangerous proclamation, but I feel that way. At least I am cured for now, that much is certain.)

I thank the heavens for my good fortune, for the grace that has been extended to me. To feel whole, healed at last. To have found happiness on both levels, and as much of ecstasy as I can bear.

Panic and Pleasure in the Third Chakra

A recent experience (rage, disempowerment, and fear at the dentist's) repeats the episode a while back after the body worker touched me slightly on my first visit and set off deep anger. Then, I went through a full round of deep emotions—fury, self-rejection, lust—each lasting a week, as if it were the selected theme for that time. The feeling centered in the solar plexus. I had diarrhea for about six weeks, and finally had to be checked for possible parasites (there were none).

This time (in the chi gong workshop), I felt the solar plexus open in ecstasy. I went through a highly similar round of feelings, but much more rapidly, each intense experience lasting only a day or so before giving way to another. Ecstasy, despair, rage—these are the key themes, the hidden motivations within this power center. (Even as I write this, my body tingles unpleasantly and the sudden stabbing pains begin. Why? What is it? Why do they come so swiftly and unexpectedly?)

Someone Defiles Sacred Ground

I went camping last weekend with Kate and Shannon at Sugarloaf Ridge. This is where I had the mystical communion with the spirit of the dead Indian brave two or so years ago. At that time, I sensed clearly that the area was sacred ground, with magical energies flowing upward from the ground. Few people were there, because it had rained on Saturday and most of the campers had left.

This was a very different experience. Someone had committed a murder and dumped the body into a ravine off the road leading right into the campground. We arrived on Friday morning, and the body was discovered that afternoon. The authorities soon established that the murder had been committed by a teenager (eighteen years old) who had killed his thirty-nine-year-old mother during an argument and disposed of her corpse in the park.

(This act seemed symbolic of the ongoing rape of the Earth so prevalent in our time—the ultimate act of sacrilege.)

Mata Amritanandamayi

What has been happening in my life? Last Friday, I went (with Alexsandra, who now also lives in San Francisco) to see Mata Amritanandamayi in Berkeley. She is an ecstatic from India, who offers *darshan* throughout the world. Thirty-nine years old, she sits on stage, singing hymns of praise *(bhakti)* to

Krishna (possibly to others). She enters a trance state, sometimes moaning or shouting "Ma . . . ma . . . ma . . ." Sometimes she "bleats" like a goat, presumably because her rapture is so intense. She is accompanied by a marvelous ensemble, most of whom are striking young men from India, playing harmonium, drums, various percussion instruments. The experience is hypnotic and rapturous. I spaced out in deep pleasure during this.

After the music, she receives the audience, one by one, in intimate embrace (hugs). The line is long, the wait tedious. I was so weary and worn out with waiting that, by the time she got to me, I was out of my earlier state of bliss. I was more concerned with doing the thing right (you had to kneel before her on your knees, because she herself was seated). In fact, you had to approach the last twenty feet or so on hands and knees, or else scoot along on your backside, all of which was extremely uncomfortable for me. I received a crushing bear hug from her, and more whispers of "Ma . . . ma . . . ma . . ." in my ear, plus a gift of one chocolate "kiss" and some flower petals. I felt little but relief once it was over, but Alexsandra said she felt wonderful vibrations.

Mata Amritanandamayi is said not only to worship but to have merged with Krishna; hence her constant emanation of love into the world. Many look on this woman as a saint, but I am wary. She is most unusual, but there is something disconcerting about her followers. Although the men look robust and even handsome, the women seem undernourished and unhappy. Further, I am mistrustful of the "enlightened ones" who have developed only the one side—the ecstatic body but not the mental (intellectual) body. I want to be able to converse with my gurus. I want them to be informed on current issues, the actual tasks before us in this world. I think we need both left brain and right brain, linear and intuitive, if we are to survive in our world.

On Meditation

Today, I will not set limits, I will not set goals. I will not say, "I will do this in order to produce that." I will not think, "Only so far can my energies go, not beyond." I will let my body become a weightless, airy being, a light-form drifting in no-space, suspended in no-time. And there, in that intersection of what is and what has never been, I will become a nonself, a knowingness beyond comprehension, surpassing cognition, a humble testimony to that which simply is.

A gentle ecstasy moves through my body, even as I write. I breathe, and a sweetness moves upward from heart, from lungs, traveling across throat. I do not know from whence this sweetness comes. Its origins, its purposes I cannot discern. Yet I allow it to breathe me; I permit my awareness to merge, to become it. This is the true breath of the heart, the suspiration of the soul.

Then I rise and make the first movement. I gently raise my arms upward in the classic opening of the chi gong practitioner. Immediately, energy stirs, and again, a gentle sweetness awakens in the chest, neck, heart, and travels down through the root chakra, then divides to descend along the inner leg, thigh and calf, to the foot. Again, I lift my hand, and become aware of the connection between the root chakra and hands. A third time, and energy traces cheek and ears. A fourth, and fifth: eye and crown chakra respond, ever so softly, grateful to be included. On the final move, I sense how everything is now awakened, each part is involved.

I move my body slowly, lifting each hand alternately, circling forward and back. More energy stirs. As I move, I rotate my hip slightly back and forth. Sweetness flows in belly and hips, as if the very bones were awakened. I moan slightly; already the pleasure is intense.

I perform the opening moves of "Embrace the Wind, Caress the Moon," one of the chi gong sequences I have learned. Energy stirs throughout; something becomes more receptive in my head, just beneath the skull. It carries a slight pain or discomfort. Here is a troubled area, where eyes often clinch and nasal passages ache. Yet today the area feels healthy, full of vitality.

I know that I put all at risk by pausing to write about it. Each interruption challenges the continuing flow. There is no guarantee that the energies, once aroused, will continue. They may withdraw, the "snake" may retreat back into his lair. Yet it seems appropriate today to take the risk. I am trying to combine, if possible, words and feeling.

I continue in a simple pattern of raising and then opening my arms. I feel the sweetness across my lower back, and along the sides of my hip bones. An even subtler vibration traces shoulder connection and, a little, in the breasts, where I almost never experience bliss. I balance carefully. I feel the effect of even the slightest shift of weight to one side or another.

This is the beginning. How the meditation will progress, how the movement will end, I do not know. Each experience is different, each pattern of feeling unique, whether it blossoms into a full ecstasy or issues as simple exercise of the physical being. Each experience is important, and must be accepted on its own terms, a gift of the invisible one who is our heavenly twin, that which is bestowed by Self to self. I return to movement, wondering if I have traded words for feeling, and if so, whether it was worth the bargain.

I pause to make a brief phone call. By the time I finish, I am in a different state of consciousness. The feelings are gone. I think it unlikely they will return today—they are like a guest who departs when the host turns away for a moment. The inner being is shy, finicky, insistent on full attention. These are its terms. We do not bargain with it. We accept its presence with gratitude (this is called grace), and in its absence, humbly await its return.

I begin again. . . . As I had feared, the ecstatic energies did not reappear. The rest of the meditation was simple movement, leading to a sense of health and well-being, but not rapture.

At the end, I did movements before the mirror. I sought to see my energies flowing and did, in fact, witness a change in my image. As so often happens, the reflection was not reassuring. The face dimmed to a dull grey, like an old negative that has lain too long in the drawer. An aura of very dark blackish purple blotted out all of my left arm, and spotted a few places on my right hand. It even showed on the tips of several fingers—I feel very good, but the aura is dull, lacking luster or vitality. I do not know what it means.

Later in the day, I visited a health club with a friend, and had a conversation with a young (twenty-five years old) teacher there. She radiates vitality and physical well being. Yet, she said, she has never felt the inner energies. Too bad, I thought, with your physical vitality, you should have marvelous experiences with the inner states. Though she exercises many hours each day, though her body is wondrously fit, she knows nothing of the inner consciousness. How ironic it is that I, straining always to maintain physical balance, constantly struggling against one symptom or another, becoming progressively slower and stiffer with age, I am the one able to feel the bliss of the body's flow, sometimes as a sweetness almost beyond my capacity to sustain.

Is There an Unspoken Agreement?

Yesterday I started with a sinus headache. For two hours I moved, massaged my feet (most painful), and did yoga and stretch exercises. Then it happened. As I sat cross-legged, swaying quietly back and forth, sweet energies flowed, mainly in the hands, up the arms, and across the top of the back. It was soft, but distinct, and deeply rapturous. Then I sat still, and with mouth closed, gently moved my tongue back and forth (a half-inch or so). Again, the exquisite energies flowed, from this most simple movement. Once more, I wonder—how can this be?

When it happens, it is as if an inner lover awakens, and accepts the little, ordinary self in mystic embrace. Is there a partnership between the incarnate self and an invisible other? Do these two work together to accomplish mysterious ends? We know only a little, hence must act on faith, accepting with gratitude what is given in the moment.

The Loneliness of the Solitary Ecstatic

This morning, I woke up in sadness and tears. I am thinking of losses, of how it is that a lover can serve as shield, to protect us against all the diminishments inflicted by the common gaze. For all others see us as distortions, mere partial reflection, of the self that we in our inmost being feel we are. Indeed, when we go out through the city, traveling on the public buses or walking with others along the streets, we lose all distinction and identity. We are simply another (in this case, aged) face, a clothed body, a moving item. The lover, more than the friend or colleague, grants us identity, acknowledges that we exist, in our most splendid aspects. The others—the friend, family (for some), associate—validate us, acknowledging our present worth and our connection to all our past selves which have been dissipated by time.

Without lover, without close friend, with no continuity achieved by occupation or group enterprise, we become invisible. We join the "Lonely Crowd," feeling ourselves nothing, the perpetual stranger.

At times, rapture alone does not sustain. Nor the sense of merger, surrender of "ego" to a higher reality. The inner voice cries out, "Why are we here, if not to know the full range of human response, its capacity to feel and love and relate to others through the common suffering? If we stay always in a state of isolation from the shared tide of experience, then why come into this world at all? Why not remain forever stranded in another realm, lost in a private cloud of ecstasy? Why bother to incarnate?"

So, the voice continues, there is more. You will be driven to make your human connections by the word, by compassionate action, by shared search. You will not be allowed to rest in your solitary bliss, your ease will be constantly broken by an urgent necessity which demands to be made visible. . . .

I am having trouble meditating this morning. The dishwasher creates too much racket in the kitchen. Next door, workmen are banging away to the background of loud radio music, so the deck is out as a quiet place. The front room is still too cold to be comfortable, but I have turned the heat on. Meanwhile, I am unsettled and jumpy.

This is the kind of day when one calls *everything* into question—one's worth, the future, the relevance of one's existence, even whether one has an existence. Strip away the externals, the lover, the relationships, the demands of occupation, involvements, and what is left? What can one cling to and call the "self"? The illusion evaporates—nothing is left but the empty center. Perhaps God can stand nothingness, but on this level, one needs something tangible to hold to, as reassurance that one is. Even the mind cannot locate its conceptual frame. One reviews the past, attempts to translate that prior reality into words. But they are pale reflections of what was then immediate experience.

Try music, says a voice within.

The Guru Appears

Then at last, after many years of searching, I found my guru. This is how it happened:

One evening, during the meditation period of my movement class, I became aware that an unknown internal face seemed to be observing me from above as I executed my personal, sacred gestures. Who was it? Next morning, I began my practice by playing a record of Tibetans chanting an "Invocation to Padmasambhava."

In my mind, I became a priest in a ceremony that in fact I seemed to follow, rather than create. In imagination, I held and then brought to life a sacred image that I presented to the (invisible) assembly. The image expanded and took its place before me, and I beheld the great master in samadhi. *He had clear features: plain rather than handsome; slender, rather young (about thirty), with shaved head, very long arms, and one shoulder exposed over his simple monk's robe. He carried no emblem or instrument. He was perfectly balanced in male and female energies (in fact, it occurred to me that if he were living today he would probably be gay). What I beheld—but more than that, what I felt—was a being of overwhelming spiritual power, a saint. His loving, sweet, powerful energies washed through me in such a way that I knew without question that I was in the presence of a holy one, and I identified with him totally.*

I felt that somehow, the deep rapture I was experiencing was a preview of and a preparation for a future time of world crisis, when many would be called upon to act as balancing centers, maintaining cosmic equilibrium in a time of acute transition. When the ceremony finished, I shrank the image and placed it in my heart.

Afterward, I read all I could find about Padmasambhava, since he was little more than a name to me. He was, I discovered (or rediscovered—surely I must have known this before) the spiritual leader who took Buddhism to Tibet. Considered the guru of gurus, he converted thousands in his time (possibly A.D. 700-800). Often he is depicted in his youthful form, and is able to appear simultaneously at several locations (hence his great ability to convert so many in a single life). In the first-level Buddhist empowerment ceremony (which I had intuitively recreated in my original kundalini initiation), I had enacted four of the prescribed five stages: ablution (for me my purifying showers, an important feature of the week); learning my true name; holding the vajra and bell; and envisioning myself as a king (when I asked if I had reached the crown chakra, I beheld myself wearing a crown).

In the traditional ceremony, the initiate is instructed to identify herself with Padmasambhava, the all-loving bodhisattva. I had omitted this feature, since I was at that time unaware of Padmasambhava, and could not construct him or call him forth from imagination. Now I had not only seen him, but had identified with him, sensing his energies flow through me.

Now this last and most powerful of all my visions was explained. My identification with him was not (as I had at first feared) a sign of inflated ego, but an instinctive following of the initiatory process. I had filled in the missing segment of the rite. My initiation was now complete.

One more vision followed a few days later. She appeared as I gazed in the mirror: a Chinese peasant woman, plain, a little coarse. She was overweight; her hair needed combing. She was, in fact, me—the unvarnished, unidealized, earthy self. She said, "When we are in our Earth-bodies, we have sex. That is what we are, what we do; but when we are in our Heaven-bodies, we expe-

rience the energies in ecstasy. That is the way it is." I think she was my "ordinary human," the part that says, "You don't have to idealize your love, or make love with a god, or surrender all your love images and focus on pure energies alone. You do not have to transcend every moment. You can sometimes simply be your human self, and act out your human needs. As human you are made of both: Heaven-body and Earth-body, equal parts."

Baba Hari Dass

Last Thursday, I drove south to a conference at Mount Madonna Center (an *ashram* on a mountain in the Santa Cruz range near Watsonville); the conference was sponsored by the "Kundalini Research Network." When I first arrived, I was lingering in the hall, waiting for dinner, when I saw a man of about sixty go by and enter a private room. He looked like somebody who had just come from work in the kitchen or on the grounds. But his features were arresting. He was slender, olive-skinned, and wore his graying hair in a ponytail. "My," I thought, "they certainly have interesting people on the staff here."

A short time later, as I stood in line for dinner, I saw through an open door a small group of people collected at the feet of a man seated at the front of the room. This man was the one I had seen a few minutes earlier. When I got my dinner tray, I carried it into that room and joined the other diners on the floor.

The man was Baba Hari Dass, the founder guru of the ashram/retreat center where the conference was being held. As I entered and took my place, he gazed at me closely. Waves of joy swept through me. After I sat, I fell into exquisite bliss, which lasted for as long as I was there. All around me, the followers were not only eating, but chatting and moving about in a lively hubbub. Baba took a tray and ate, sometimes stopping to hear questions from those who approached him. He has taken a vow of silence, so he answered by writing on a small slate board he carries with him. The bliss I experienced was a deep rapture, beginning in the heart and traveling upward into the head (although my head was not completely opened, as in my original experience). I remained in this state until he left the room.

Next evening, as I stood in line for dinner, I felt rapturous waves sweep my body from crown to toe. I looked up and realized that, once more, Baba was holding *satsang* in the adjacent room. I didn't bother to pick up food, but entered and immediately fell into a state of ecstasy, amid the clamor and movement of the residents, many of whom had brought their children.

On Saturday, I went in a third time. This time, there was bliss, but not as much as before. Baba seemed to be focused more on the questioners, and on playing with and teasing the children.

I also experienced great bliss during the first meditation class offered by Sarasvati, one of his longtime students. This experience consisted primarily of performing the four yogic purification practices *(pranayama)*. Each time I sucked in my diaphragm or expelled my breath in short gusts, I felt exquisite rushes of pleasure. I went to the class a second time on Saturday, but the bliss was much less intense.

Whence comes this bliss? I have experienced such feelings many, many times, during my own practice, especially when the "inner lover" manifests; or in classes that involve music or chanting or group meditation; or sometimes when I am with a spiritually evolved group, at a workshop or conference, where there is frequently a deep flow of blissful energy.

I do not think I have ever had an experience in which merely sitting with a holy one had such an effect. (Of course, the followers contributed energy and "vibrations.") I am deeply drawn to him—perhaps this experience is akin to *shaktipat,* the Divine Energy that the guru may deliberately transmit to the follower in a ceremony of initiation. Or perhaps he actually gave me *shaktipat*—if so, it was a very familiar vibration. Does this mean that he and I derive from the same source (tradition)? Or does it signify that the guru sets your own inner frequency in motion and that you experience it according to your own nature?

In any event, I was much surprised, for I found that I deeply loved this man, and would be content to remain in his presence always. Yet, at the same time, I feel I have something to give in exchange. I am unwilling to be cast in the role of passive recipient. What I want is for him to recognize me as someone he knew in a remote past—perhaps as teacher or friend, someone now returned in a very different guise. I would be angry if he treated me like any beginner, though in some ways that is exactly what I am. And I want him to talk to me. I do not see the logic of his vow. What does it accomplish? I think it is merely an irritating impediment, a self-indulgence, rather than a self-discipline. But then, I am no guru. And for me, he needs no words.

Clearly, this is the "sweet fire" that Rumi often speaks of. What would it be like to know this divine energy on a constant basis? I both desire and fear this experience. I do not wish to feel that my own inner sensations are so dependent on the presence of another being. I want to be the spiritual leader, the one who gives *shaktipat*. But of course, I am in no way prepared, since my own energies are so unpredictable, and since I have not undergone the necessary disciplines to attain this higher state. Something in me is irresistibly drawn toward him, and something else strongly objects to giving up so much personal power to another human. How would he treat me?

On Tuesday, I took a yoga lesson at the Integral Yoga Center, whose guru is Swami Satchidananda. The teacher was much concerned that I performed the *asanas* so poorly. She kept trying to "help" me by correcting me, or coming over to observe me more closely, or having me stop to see how the others were doing the postures. Finally, she asked if I had confused this class with another, one designed for those unable to do the regular beginner's class. So I asked her if she wanted me to leave. She said no, and didn't bother me thereafter. Afterward, I told her that I often feel the energies deeply, even though I cannot do the *asanas* very well. I showed her how I can sometimes feel incredible bliss just by moving my fingers. She appeared to understand, but I feel she showed great insensitivity in the class by singling me out. Once again, I am not successful when I try to connect with an established center as a student.

Baba Hari Dass is the only spiritual leader I have discovered who inspires me to pursue the connection.

Doubting the Doubter

Like all who have endured some overwhelming experience, who have been ravished by a transcendental revelation, I am essentially ruined for critical inquiry, for rational investigation of conflicting perspectives. No matter how convincing the argument, how irrefutable the evidence, I always hold back, tongue in cheek, convinced of knowledge beyond the evident, of truth lying under the surface of the observable.

Yet at times, I doubt the doubter, challenge the inner skeptic: how can this one transparent moment be true in a world of relativity? How can this single personal reception of grace contradict the witness of the common mind?

Concreteness

More concreteness, is the cry. More particulars (what Henry James called the "solidity of specification") to make it real. But something inside resists. Doesn't want to locate me at a center, doesn't wish to detail this rocking chair, the surrounding scene in my mother's room, the birthday flowers, the comical clown doll with its absurd lavender curls, the shelf with its display of hopelessly out-of-date family photographs, some dead, all changed, forgotten selves who once inhabited a lost world.

Why? Because something inside fears to commit. It knows that just as the "past," with all its fragments and crystallized moments dissolved into the rushing stream of "that which was," so this present moment deludes us with the seemingly real. It knows that if we pause to name, catalog, enumerate, we may be captured and held, forever imprisoned in this fantasy world, whose allurements and seductions we eternally resist. We will not give way to the interplay of imagery. We hold our breath, eternally. We do not succumb, and remain forever a potential, an unrealized possibility, a consciousness which never fully enters creation.

God Again

Maybe God is a boundless energy source that requires embodiment in the material to experience its own rapture, just as the sound wave that must hit a target (an ear?) and echo back in order to become audible noise. Otherwise, there are only the vibrations rushing through empty space, never passing to where there are things seen, things heard, sensations felt. Maybe this is what God wants—to extend its range of experience through incarnation in the embodied and responsive universe.

Perhaps God engages in an unending "drug trip," a perpetual experiment in various states of consciousness, from the mineral through the full spectrum of awareness of animal, human, angelic. We view the deity and long to merge with that unbounded awareness. The divine likewise covets our condition of limited but incredibly rich engagement with our surrounding environment. Through us, God plays at imaginary responses to illusory stimuli. The seen, the heard, the felt—all are simply the infinite vibrations narrowed and concentrated so as to be apprehensible to our limited capacities. Through us, God discovers how it would be to be other than a field of infinite, extending potency.

We seek God endlessly because we hunger to know our source. God pursues us relentlessly, because through us divinity experiences its own inherent nature. Perhaps God is a perpetual orgasm, whose massive feeling waves roll ecstatically and unceasingly through the universe. Whoever feels, knows God. God wants me to feel something, and then to say what I feel.

God as Lover

Kundalini is pleasure translated from the loins to the head. As long as the sensation is located in the genitals, it remains primarily a transaction between humans, or at least an event on the human level, with God as the third party, the onlooker. But once the feeling is lifted to the crown, God becomes both lover and beloved, ravisher and ravished. Other forms of divine love are possible, but this is the consummation, realized by the human partner here on this side of the eternal. Everyone will know it, once the body drops at death. It is a bliss that does not rely on flesh, but derives from the merger of consciousness with consciousness, when the finite is reclaimed by the divine.

Of all the metaphors for God, that of lover is the most challenging, and the most rewarding, if attained.

A Native American Initiation, a *Kriya*, and Chanting

Recently I experienced an unexpected "inner initiation" into Native American mysteries. I got an Indian name ("Sky-Flying Woman") and received (an imaged) blanket, pipe, and feathered headdress. I saw three faces: a young (twenty-something) man with headband and feathers, who escorted me to an older wise man in his mid-forties who performed the initiation. I also saw an ancient wise woman with the face of the little old Latina who lives around the corner here in a building where many Hispanic families crowd together.

Then Alexsandra and I went to the first breath workshop offered by students of Panditji (Ravi Shankar). Their group is called the "Art of Conscious Living." We introduced ourselves and did a few breathing exercises. On the next day, we performed yoga stretching, listened to a lecture from Mar (one of the leaders), and practiced breathing. This was followed by the *Kriya*, the breathing exercise that we had heard so much about. It was reported to be incredibly transformative. The exercise involved thirty to forty minutes of deep breathing, in varying rhythms, from slow to extremely rapid. It was quite taxing, and I was afraid I would not make it through, but I managed to hang on until the end. I felt enlivened and vitalized, in the sense of feeling quite healthy and whole. So, I thought, this *Kriya* makes you feel stronger, but does not offer any of the bliss I so frequently experience.

Then on the third day everything changed. From the first moment, the room was charged with rapture. Each tiny yoga movement produced strong sensuous currents throughout the body. The *Kriya* (which we repeated) brought me near to rapture, but I never went completely over. It was a kind of intense, even fierce, dynamic bliss. At times, I approached the edges of a deep grief. During the rest period afterward, my body felt alive, awakened into bliss. I felt a line of rapturous energy flowing across the soles of my feet, from toes to ankle, then moving up my legs and then finally diffusing in delight throughout my body. I was "blissed out."

I was pleased to find that I could endure the intense breathing without losing inner balance. My energies responded nicely throughout, even when some in the group were noisy. These *siddhas* (advanced students of Transcendental Meditation) apparently went into spontaneous "flying" (springing up a few inches in cross-legged position—the ancient texts describe it as "hopping like frogs.") There was much bumping and thumping as they came back down. I did not panic at these strange sounds, but continued on my own path, undisturbed. So perhaps I am finally finished (or almost) with kundalini instability. (It took Gopi Krishna twelve years, and I am in my twelfth year now.)

I heard Alexsandra thump, but I never saw her go up from the ground. She said later that she did not simply feel bliss, but that she was bliss. She also saw a deep golden light within her.

I also attended Jill Purce's five-day workshop on chanting. In one of the workshop exercises we each sang or chanted the name of our matriarchal line (mother, grandmother, etc.) as far back as we could go. We forgave them, and gave each a mental gift, receiving a gift in return. Then we did the same for the patriarchal line. Strangely, I felt a strong vibration from my father's father, whom I barely knew, and sensed that I shared his energies, though we expressed them differently. He was a character, a bit of a show-off, a storyteller in the old oral tradition. He ended his days as a folk medicine man, peddling mysterious remedies to his clients.

I realized how great the barrier is between parent and child when homosexuality is involved. How we (the children) wear heavy armor to dull our feelings and mask our need for love, how we must do this in order to survive. How we must always pretend to be other than we are. I shed a few tears at this point, though crying is very difficult for me.

Picking Up Energies from Others

On Saturday, I noticed two things. Once, when a friend came in, I felt something akin to pain in the subtle body. I must tense up around her, or else pick up her tension. Later, when C. and I went to an exhibit at the art museum, I felt my aura brighten and fill with delightful energy. Again, tension blocks and brings pain. Relaxation and pleasure open and yield pleasure. But the process has become so subtle now. Is this the mode of the future? Will I be able to live with it?

Somewhere in my reading, I recall testimony that among the bands of spirits, nothing is hidden or private. They live in harmony, because what affects one affects all. Therefore it is disastrous to entertain negative feelings toward one another, since these immediately are known and are turned back on oneself. Likewise, the group shares a harmonious state based on group well-being.

Somehow, as my system gets fine-tuned, I feel as if I am moving toward some such state of vulnerability to surrounding circumstances, for good or ill. Yet in other respects I have learned to defend myself against the fierce waves of hostility and/or suffering that emanate from many of the city dwellers. I am even at ease in the midst of chaotic and sometimes even conflicting energies of various groups, such as the passengers on a bus, or a crowd milling on the sidewalk. I can walk down Mission Street, with its surging tides of immigrants, noise and chaos, dirty sidewalks and desperate poor, without having my energies go berserk, as they often used to.

This morning, once more, my stomach was off and I could do only a little practice. How exquisite the energies feel when the flow is unobstructed and the balance is maintained. How agonizing the pain when the body is "ill."

If I could only keep my stomach settled, perhaps I could have ecstatic practices every day. Related to this, one night recently, my subtle body was in a state of pleasant arousal (during sleep). I coughed, and felt the sweet energies explode softly throughout my system. What next?

Lunch with Friends

Yesterday I had lunch with Jouida and Jan. We got into a prolonged discussion over whether a consciousness revolution was occurring now in the late 1990s. Jan thinks not, that there have always been people around with advanced consciousness, that times of opening (as the Greek Golden Age or the Romantic period of Europe) are followed by times of darkness and chaos. She points out that the world appears to be growing worse, not better (war, poverty, crime, horror, environmental pollution). I agree with the facts she brought forth, but posed the counterargument (the crisis is greater now, so the transformation will be deeper; the great change is just beginning, and will increase incrementally).

Even as I spoke, I drifted into another state, in which Jan and Jouida looked lovely. I felt a strong identification with them and the surrounding colors deepened. We ate at a restaurant run by recovering addicts as a money-raiser for their residential home. Perhaps there is an atmosphere of love there that shaped my consciousness that day.

Anger

Once more, I am ill with acute stomach disorder. This is like Sisyphus and the stone: a little progress, and then defeat once again. I am reminded of my mother's journals, which consisted to a great extent of how she felt each day, the causes, the concerns, the domestic contretemps that brought on each spell of illness.

I think the physical state issues from a great well of feeling that has been stopped for so long in my life, primarily from the rigid boundaries I placed on my relationship with parents to spare them the knowledge of who I truly was. I also experienced much social constriction from playing as best I could a role that society imposed, carefully avoiding infringements, disclosure— these armorings take their toll.

This and the inability to stand up in intimate relationship. The disappointment at never being confirmed or encouraged in any creative or spiritual endeavor. The sense of always having to react to another's desire or need. The inability to express true feelings, especially if these are negative or disagreeing. The fear of upsetting another. The lack of true creative or loving outlet. The loss of a loving relationship in life. The lack of the intimacy in relationship. The loss of the friend-lover. The lack of sexual partner. Of spiritual partner. The inability to express personal desire or will. The lack of a project, an ongoing project shared with others. The absence of a coherent, continuing identity. Lack of recognition as a person of talent, worth, or value. Not having a place. Not knowing who or what I am. Not being able to act, to move to a new location, to cut loose from what entangles me. Not being able to remove myself from distressing circumstances.

Would I prosper if I picked up and left? Would I emerge into an equally distressing situation, marked by loneliness, isolation, despair? Should I hang on here to reap such benefits as have accrued over the years? Is my stomach pain an expression of frustration (creative, personal, sexual) or is it merely physical?

Again, I feel anger. Deep burning anger for the sum total of the repressed feelings, blocked-up energies, and thwarted movements of my life. I am tired of witnessing other people's creative achievements. I am weary of being an audience for others. I want to enact *my* gestures, perform *my* rituals, come forth on my terms, display my features. I wish to be the person I am. This pain derives from, indeed is, rage. Arising from all that has been held back, tied down, not expressed. It will out, whether or no. And part of the anger is that there is no one to help, no one to act as guide, protector, to carry me through.

After twenty minutes of noisemaking and movement, I feel better. I feel improved for now at least. Surely I must find a way to break through, to link the inner and outer life.

In this above entry, I tried to name and release as many of the sources of my anger as I could. I then did a series of exercises to express anger—I made angry sounds, did angry gestures, made angry faces, for twenty minutes or so. I was, in fact, dealing with unresolved psychological issues, which the kundalini was uncovering and forcing into full consciousness. After the kundalini is awakened, all these hidden tensions and held memories of trauma or hurt must be addressed as part of the cleansing process. Until this healing occurs, forward progress is difficult. Even established meditators or advanced students of body disciplines such as the martial arts may have to focus on repair of inner wounds before they can go forward.

Composing Poetry in My Sleep

Last night my dog woke me about 5 A.M. As I wakened, I realized that I was composing (or channeling) poetry in my sleep. It was coming very fast. The first two were fully developed poems (but I did not remember them). The last one was something like:

O Sakyamuni . . .
O Sakyamuni . . .
O Sakyamuni . . .
When will you hear my call?

In the dream, I was writing these lines down quite fast in my notebook, but I ran out of space, as I am now doing in this one. Then I had two additional strange dreams, one about a young man who acted out his feelings in poses, as if he were a piece of shifting sculpture; another about a young woman whose emotions came through her as electric shocks (I felt these as I dreamed).

My Mantra

Recently, I read that the name *Ram* was the mantra most commonly given to beginners. Is this why my mantra, which came to me a few years after I rejected the one from TM, is based on this name for god (which at first I did not recognize as such)?

Sri Rama, Rama,
Sri Rama, Rama,
Sri Rama, Rama,
Sri . . .

I have always loved these syllables, even before I knew their meaning. At first, I discovered that *Sri* was a term of respect, such as in the name of Bhagwan Shree Rajneesh. Later I realized that *Ram* (or *Rama*) was the name of a god; apparently it is a name for the highest of all, or so I choose to believe.

When I tried to repeat the mantra given to me by my TM initiator, it seemed to break open my head with pain. I was distressed and even made ill by it. But these syllables (a gift from the inner teacher) bring joy and union.

The Emergence of the New Humanity

Kundalini is the release into the world of ultimate feeling. It is the connection to the world within the familiar, the realms below and inside that which we usually know. Kundalini confirms for us that we exist, and that we exist as streams of rapture. The energy of the infinite is also the energy of the local self. It affords us a new way of experiencing our being, not as consciousness, segregated and separated from body, but as awareness contained in and fused with flesh. It exposes the Platonic lie of the separation of matter and spirit, and it heals the Cartesian split. Mind and body are one, a single pulsing, reacting organism, capable of experiencing both pleasure and pain at the most refined levels of sensation.

Kundalini unites body and spirit, and reveals that the *subtle* body informs our existence as much as the physical. So, when we meld body and spirit, we are talking not just about flesh and awareness, but about that which is located at a midrange, which is neither and both, mysterious and familiar, yet intrinsic to our makeup.

Why explore the subtle body? Why play with these delicate energies, discover the chakras, open the "third eye"? To know ourselves more, to reclaim that which has been denied in the long interval of the mind-body split, to confirm that here, in the flesh itself, the incarnate spirit resides still bearing marks of its divine origin.

Kundalini is the goddess. The goddess is Kundalini. To deny one is to reject the other and to consign feeling, flesh, and the energy that binds them to the realm of all that remains unknown because it is withheld from consciousness. To accept kundalini is to say yes to the Mother, to the body in its delicate manifestations, and to open to the delight of the universal energies, to embrace the Earth and its many inhabitants, and to know oneself allied with all creatures and beings, alive or discarnate, everything caught in the divine spectacle of *lila*, the never-ending mind play of the god.

Andrew Harvey

When I discovered Andrew Harvey's book, Hidden Journey, *I immediately bought copies for my friends. Here, at last, was a deep mystic, one steeped in Western and Eastern modes, who presented his spiritual awakening in a delicately written, lovingly structured prose. Finally, I thought, a writer worthy of the task, one whose craft matches the revelation.*

So when I heard that Harvey was arriving in San Francisco to teach at a local college, I felt it was a unique opportunity for me. I enrolled in his class on Rumi, which began in April. The classroom was packed, with students spilling onto the floor and into the halls. Would he be a proper English academic, wearing tweeds and carrying a pipe? Would he be a wild-eyed ecstatic, babbling incoherently of his otherworldly adventures?

Yesterday afternoon, Andrew Harvey gave his opening lecture on Rumi. It was unlike any verbal experience I have ever had, that is, not that the words themselves were strange (indeed, they were beautiful), but the overall *effect* of the presentation was striking. Harvey radiates dynamic, divine energy. He is a man passionately committed to his subject (Rumi and the path of spiritual transformation), and is unafraid to show that passion. He announced at the beginning that he would teach not as a scholar or poet (both of which he is), but as a devotee of Rumi. He is witty, sophisticated, intense, present, and profoundly inspired. He is androgynous, a beautiful blend of male and female. He is tall, slender, and graceful. He is feminine without being effeminate. He is exceedingly bright.

He wants to get Rumi's message to the world. When he entered the room, his first act was to write this on the board:

Only the fire eaters find the light.
Love is the flame which when it blazes
burns away everything except the beloved.

As I write up this entry, images and line of poetry occur:

How ashamed I am of my insufficiency.
How earnestly abject
at my appalling inconsequence.
Why do I prate of poetry
when real poets
listen to god in silence?

Harvey said that he had twice heard the music of the universe. He mentioned that he had left a lover behind in Paris, so perhaps he has not taken a vow of celibacy. When Harvey was a small child in India, he was taken to visit the Taj Mahal. This was a profound and (I think) prophetic experience for him, the ultimate expression of love to Love (It is clear that this has become the dominant motif of his life). When he reads the class a passage of poetry, he does not launch into a critical dissection, but tells us to sit in silence a few minutes to meditate on the poem. How wonderful! How amazing!

Basking in the Glow

Today, I continue to bask in the glow of the experience with Harvey. At first I was excited, talking at length to all who would listen, calling up friends to announce my find. Now something has quieted within me. I feel not urgency but a calmer sense of satisfaction, completion, as if something that has undergone a long preparation has happened. I have a greater steadiness inside, as if he is (or represents) that which I have been seeking and needing.

Why should I desire some guru when I have Harvey as a teacher? Indeed—what need have I of any human mediator for the divine when I have the inner guide who has led me so long? The answer: I am lonely and need *some* companionship, *some* confirmation of the path. I need a stimulus, a push in a particular direction, to begin a life of actively giving back some of the gifts which have been granted me. Who is Andrew Harvey? Is he a reality, or did I dream him up from the depths of my soul? I am trying to be reasonable about all this, but Harvey is beautiful, intelligent, in love with poetry and all art, wonderfully articulate and expressive, and deeply spiritual, so why wouldn't I be fascinated by him?

He has his work, his tasks, his assignments. And I sit here in San Francisco, writing in this notebook that no one reads, going to lectures, taking chi gong, practicing my *pranayama* and Taoist movements, experiencing my bliss, discovering pain, looking with wonder and despair at the city with its splendor and pain.

Today as I moved through the crowds or rode the streetcar, everyone seemed to shine with a certain internal beauty. Colors were bright, precise, as if my head was in a state of solid balance. This is not the first time I have experienced this state, but it is the first that has arisen from merely being with a teacher in a classroom.

Harvey's Second Class

Yesterday was the second class of Andrew Harvey. The room was even more crowded than before. Even floor space was scarce—obviously, word has traveled. Harvey talked this time of the stages of initiation and of Rumi's life up to his meeting with Shams (the strange wandering mystic who initiated Rumi by instant transmission).

Harvey wrote on the board:

I was raw.
Then I got cooked.
Now I am burned.

Harvey then described the four stages of the mystical journey: childhood, the creation of the false self, the destruction of the false self, and enlightenment. In the third stage, the spirit encounters much suffering as well as joy. Few are prepared to sacrifice all for the Divine Light. In the final stage, the Divine Self and the human self join. Only a handful arrive at this ultimate destination.

Harvey is passionate, dramatic, even theatrical in his presentation. He seeks to bring each listener into the circle of flame, to torch each heart, ignite each cell. I have known bliss in chanting, movement, and breath. I have been invaded by ecstasy before the silent Baba Hari Dass. But this is the first time presence has been accompanied by such transcendent speech (eloquent, wise, utterly perceptive). The language obviously flows from Harvey's core.

Will I have the courage to ask to speak with him?

Bliss in the Street, Rapture while Eating

Yesterday, again, I experienced much intense, sensuous pulsation while I was eating lunch with Kate in a cafe, walking on the sidewalk, or waiting for her in a sunlit passageway. I felt a strong ecstasy well up from the soles of my feet, through my wrists and elbows, chest, head—everywhere. Once more, everything was shimmering with that deep radiance as if the world had just been made and everything reflected the perfection of newness. *Clearly, my senses have been awakened and my energies aroused by the inspiration of Harvey's class.*

But yesterday evening and again this morning I felt ill again, as if with rheumatism or arthritis. Two allergy pills seemed to help. Once more, I am reminded of the system's acute sensitivity to *both* pleasure and pain, and given evidence of the delicate balance between them.

Upwellings of Creativity

It is if an intentional process is going on, under and within, around and through, sweeping us to ends as yet invisible and indeterminable, although inexorable and inevitable. We experience the process only in bits and pieces, as fleeting explosions, brief flashes that are chaotic, disruptive, annihilating. We are carried headlong in a frail rubber raft, dashed and swirled by raging waters, on a river whose source we don't know and whose final end we cannot see. We imagine this—the raft, our interactions with one another within this universe that is our field of action—to be the cause and origin of the events that we experience and seemingly precipitate. We bob up and down, this way and that, on a stream of chaos.

Perhaps we are drowning, and can survive only by learning to breathe the water. We cannot force our will upon this wild current. We can only align ourselves, cease our strivings to control, and allow its unpredictable rhythms to penetrate and retune our entire being.

Kundalini, *shaktipat,* the sweet fire of the inner energies, are ways of experiencing the divine creativity. In these states of transcendence, or *samadhic* bliss, we feel God imaged as the divine lover, or angelic presence, or cosmic bliss bringer enter us, allowing us a taste of the divine essence of which the universe is composed. Too much, and we are annihilated; too little, and we are frozen into plasticized automatons imagining they are alive.

The ancient seers, the yogis, the great mystic poets (such as Rumi and Kabir), even the soothsayers and alchemists—have kept alive for us the memory of our unique origin. They have, through the ages, written the hidden history of the human spirit. In a sense, all of this—the practice of yogic bliss as well as the performance of sacred rites in secret places—has been preparation for the present moment. For now once more the sacred is entering human history. As time and timelessness prepare for their crucial intersection, the hidden is again made manifest, the occult opened to light.

In one sense, the deepest psychic experiences, the numinous eruptions of singularity and novelty in our personal lives, are not ours at all. They are upwellings of the divine creativity, possible when we still the little, local mind. This is why we refer to the essential death of ego or spiritual annihilation that must occur before valid inner initiation or visionary experience can transpire. When we get ourselves out of the way—through personal trauma, or unexpected life events, or even some drugs—the within can emerge, enact its sacred drama on its own hidden stage which we, if sufficiently privileged, may later recall and (mistakenly) identify as our own. Act, actor, and witness all are now one—ourselves temporarily merged with, enfolded into, the divine performance.

On Drugs, Sex, and Mystical Union

One pioneer in the field of shamanic vision insists that psychedelics and communal sex are essential to "dissolve the boundaries" of ego and self. How sad that he obviously is unaware of (or has no capacity for) meditation as a way to dispel the illusion of separate selfhood and release the awareness into blissful union.

He is correct that we (humanity) need ecstasy in our repertory of experience. But he is oblivious to or deliberately ignores the reality of the transcendent mystic state, achieved without drugs or violent chemical disruption of the normal nervous response system.

Has he read Rumi? Does he know what kundalini is capable of? Is his system too scarred by heavy drug use to respond to more subtle stimuli? Has he noticed the damaging effects on our world of the massive drug experiments of the last twenty years? He speaks as if experimentation with drugs were a novel suggestion, an experience to be tried, rather than acknowledging that for far too many it is a project that has disastrously failed.

Although I had been a teacher of English literature for many years, I only now began to grasp the deep connection between sacred verse and the sacred energies. With Rumi, Kabir, Hafiz, and others to guide me, I began to write poetry that sprang out of and reflected much of my own journey. The growing popularity of such writing today reveals the deep hunger of the human spirit for contact with the Transcendent, a need too often ignored or denied in our time. Kundalini energy is in fact seen by many as the deep wellspring from which much creativity proceeds. The great masters of ecstatic verse are like conduits through whom God speaks to God.

More Dreams of Reunion

This week has been quieter. Less rapture, less of the "shining brilliance." I am focusing on developing steadiness and inner strength. I continue to have dreams of reunion and (at times) reconciliation with various persons from my past, some very minor, even people I knew only slightly in childhood, whom I had all but forgotten.

Baba Hari Dass and the Rapture of Raptures

Yesterday, I drove to Santa Cruz with my friend Helen to experience *satsang* with Baba Hari Dass at the Pacific Cultural Center. It has been almost a year since my first encounter with him.

The Pacific Cultural Center is a pleasant, church-like building located in a residential section of Santa Cruz. The day was mild, the sun shining. We arrived about an hour early, for the drive down took less time than I had anticipated. I had felt a bit queasy, a little off during the drive, and wondered if the experience here would fall flat.

When we entered the main room, it was almost empty. I paused to look through some books and literature displayed on a table near the door. As I leafed through one book (which contained many pictures of Baba), I became aware of sweet sensations flowing within me. These were a gentle foreshadowing of what was to follow.

The *satsang* included music (by an instrumental ensemble), chanting (from the Bhagavad Gita), silent meditation, prayer, and answers (written on his slate) by Baba to questions presented by the audience. He also accepted several gifts from children of attendees.

Almost as soon as the *kirtan* (devotional singing in Sanskrit) started, I sensed exquisite energies flowing in my head, and under my skull, as if a flower (I imaged a lotus) were pressing upward. Soon these energies swept downward into my chest and arms. As the music continued, I began to throb with a bliss of a texture unlike any I have before experienced. The feelings grew in intensity until I experienced what for me seemed to be the "rapture of raptures," the ecstasy of ecstasies. Many times Baba looked at me and sometimes I looked back, when I was able to open my eyes. At times I remember looking up and moving my eyes (which were closed) back and forth or rotating them as sweet waves swept back and forth across and under my skull. At times my heart seemed pierced by excruciating bliss. Sometimes I thought I must lose consciousness, or at least immediate awareness of my surroundings.

Once (when I had my eyes closed), I thought I felt Baba's presence much closer, almost in front of me. I thought perhaps he had sent his spirit from the front of the room to stand before me; then I opened my eyes and saw that Baba was no longer sitting in front of us. He had left the room (temporarily), and had passed near me as he exited.

The rapture continued to be extremely intense during the ritual chanting of the Bhagavad Gita. Each syllable, each microsound, awakened ever more subtle and refined sensations, fluctuating and pulsing throughout the torso and head, the hands and shoulders, at times even traveling into the soles of my feet. Sometimes I wondered how much I could sustain, but I always seemed to be ready for more.

Once I seemed to communicate telepathically with Baba. When he asked mentally, "What do you want from me?" I answered (silently), "To love you and be loved by you. To receive help in finding my life direction, and do the thing I am supposed to be doing in this life."

At times I felt my aura expand far beyond its usual limits. I saw a few images during this experience: A female Indian guru flickered briefly in my mind's eye, and then, to my surprise, Sri Aurobindo appeared. But even before these, came an image of Christ on the cross (the last image of my original initiation through kundalini). This Christ figure was slightly muscular, not the languid, soft being we so often image. Once during this experience, I seemed to become Krishna himself, in radiant splendor.

Later, Baba answered several questions (using his slate and an interpreter) after the *kirtan* and chanting. Most were quite elementary. The askers were young, and had not thought much about spiritual matters. One asked how to get rid of a curse. Baba answered, "I don't know." I found this an excellent reply.

Afterward, Helen and I sat down at a table in the larger room to eat lunch. As Baba left, he paused briefly at our table to give me time to turn and face him. I bowed and smiled and he did likewise.

What is going on here? Is this the usual experience of one who receives *shaktipat?* Do lots of people feel these "vibrations" from him? Is it in any way personal? Is this a special meeting or just a guru fishing for followers? I don't know. I really don't care. Afterward, I felt that I had been ravished. I was overwhelmed. My kundalini had first awakened twelve years ago, almost to the day. Often in past years, intense experiences have occurred on or around this date, as if an anniversary were being celebrated. What a birthday party!

A Devotional Retreat

Next I went to Mount Madonna (Baba's ashram, named for its location) to take part in a devotional retreat. About fifty of us participated. Most of the first night and the following day were spent in explanation and instruction: how to do *pranayama,* what a mantra is. We did a little practice, but there were many interruptions to explain; apart from the *kirtan,* there was little to inspire or lift the spirit. The food was good, the weather excellent, the company pleasant. I thought, "Well, this is a fine vacation, even if the transcendent element is missing."

Then on Saturday it all began. I went into an altered state and took deep bliss from virtually every part of the day, from the ritual *arati* (fire ceremony to awaken Krishna, to bring his spirit into presence among us), to the hours of Sanskrit chanting of the *Bhagavad Gita, pranayama,* and other practices. Again the *kirtan* (music) was ecstatic; again, I felt as though I had stumbled into Heaven, that perhaps this ashram was my true home.

Most of the questions to Baba had to do with moral attitudes and behavior, particularly with reference to sex or the acceptability of suicide. His answers were clear, to the point, and for the most part, what we might expect from a devout, dedicated renunciate who wishes to give his "flock" sound precepts for living. Some questions had to do with sin, or maintaining the discipline of practice; others were about reincarnation and dreams.

After careful thought, I submitted the following question (anonymously): "Sometimes in spiritual practice, ecstatic feelings arise in the body, as, for example, the heart, head, and hands. When this happens, should the student seek counsel from the teacher or bear the ecstasy in silence?"

Answer: "In spiritual practice, these things happen. It may be a sign of progress. However, there is a danger of getting fixated on them. Also, there is danger they will become sensual. Go beyond them."

So Baba Hari Dass (whose name I found out at last, means "Servant of God") does not endorse or encourage ecstasy as part of the spiritual path. He focuses on moral and physical "purity." And ethics. The yogic practices (*asana, pranayama,* chanting, ritual) open and awaken the energy centers. But never is the connection between these two levels (spirit and body) explored or made clear. If we wish to connect with God in a mental, nonmaterial way, why bother to learn these techniques? If we simply want to feel good physically, who worry about the moral imperatives?

What is "bliss of yogic union" if not a *felt flow* of rapture throughout the system, the divine piercing of the body, God essence entering every cell in an intimate merging. How can we be one and not know it? How can we come to God if we do not open—totally, in every particular, in all dimensions—to the lover within?

Is this denial of the body's role (the subtle body, that is) more patriarchal condemnation of the Feminine, of the realm of feelings, joy, rapture? Does it reflect the male fear that he will somehow go out of control, his reverence giving way to sensual passion? Is there a thin line between sensual (sexual) and sensuous (sensed, felt)? What do we make of the "passion" of Saint Teresa, the blade of love piercing her heart, her face rapt in near-orgasmic trance? What were the great saints of India—the Kabirs, the Mirabais, and their ilk—celebrating in their love songs if not their state of amorous adoration of the divine? Why did Rama Krishna go into overwhelming ecstasy when he tried to explain his state of mind to the world? Why did Rumi dance for weeks after the disappearance of Shams? Surely his energies were raised to the highest pitch, reaching an intensity that demanded some release via the body's movement?

These admonitions to "slay the feelings" awaken uncomfortable reminders of the Puritans inveighing against the flesh—and they included in this sphere *all* art, beauty, ornament, movement, dancing. Are we back to Gnostic rejection of the flesh as inherently evil because it takes us out of the realm of pure thought and immerses us in the base plane of elemental feeling? Are we unable to make a distinction between a pleasure that is a fleshy thrill and a bliss that is a grace from God? Can we not discern the difference between that which primarily arouses us to sexual pursuit and what begets in us the deepest love for God, and all other beings—which in fact reveals to us the scale on which we are embraced, thus enabling us to perceive our common identity with all humankind, whom we likewise reverence and adore?

Finally, if we are to undergo transformation at the cellular level, will our cells not speak to us? Is not our private joy a minuscule taste of the ongoing cosmic rapture in which the divine is not involved but rather is the continuing reality, the actual essence? Who are we to reject the graces the unknown has bestowed upon us? We had to defy the unspoken prohibitions of the parent to achieve initiation of the flesh. Now must we disregard the strictures of an overcautious, sense-denying religious authority to attain initiation of the spirit?

Today in meditation I saw an image of a corset: an old-fashioned, straitlaced gadget, designed to hold down and repress all the body's natural capacities, even the breath. I realized (with gratitude) that I was having none of it. I would follow my own path, even if it led straight to Hades (which it doesn't, believe me, unless one is unable to tell the difference between higher and lower realms). I want to maintain contact with this, the more usual, more ordinary mode of being, one which does not squelch the feeling aspect of self. I do not want to climb to Heaven on the broken remnants of the senses.

I am not (never was) wanton, riotous, orgiastic. Quite the contrary, it has taken me a lifetime to contact this secret realm of the inner self, in which body and spirit conspire together, fusing into a unit of knowing that is neither one nor the other, but a new organ of consciousness. *The world is vibration,* and I am that thing that allows and knows this divine energy as it streams into and through me, for I and it are of the same order of being. Who wants a passionless existence? Isn't it better to allow the throb of bliss in the heart, to know love as part of a shared resonance, to *feel* the oneness with all which is external to self? Sometimes I wonder if the refusal to feel arises out of the control needs of the experiencer? Or perhaps it is the consolation of those who have passed beyond this state (of feeling) into a less body-inclusive condition. I am reminded of old men who urge youth to be celibate. Or libertines who say "Aha!" and wink when a prim maiden takes an innocent turn on the dance floor.

Those whose senses need reigning in, let them buy halters. For the rest of us, let us move forward freely, welcoming what awaits as well as the journey there. The key, here, as always, is to attain balance. Neither Wagner's *Ride of the Valkyries* nor the prim Preludes of Chopin, but something strong, active, real, affirming and connecting self, other, world.

Despite my almost irresistible attraction to Baba Hari Dass, I did not become a disciple. Something in me clung to the connection with my inner guru, who had led me so expertly through my difficult journey. I visited Baba's ashram once or twice again, but did not pursue a more intimate personal connection.

The *Gayatri Mantra*, Music, and Other Practices

Since so many whom I have asked disdained ecstasy, labeling it a distraction that might easily lead to sensuality, I have scrupulously avoided experiencing it. But today (my third day at home after two weeks in Oklahoma and Kansas) I played a tape of a Sanskrit mantra (Vyaas Houston intoning the *Gayatri Mantra*) and *immediately* felt sweet, extremely high energies rouse in my upper body.

I sometimes think I am the only person in the world exploring these states. *No one,* even presumed experts, seems to be sufficiently familiar with them to counsel or guide me. *Where is the teacher?*

Of course, the inner guru takes over and does it all. I am merely the vessel of "his" reality during these sessions. (I sense my inner guru as "he.") He seems ready, waiting, receptive, entering almost instantaneously when an opening occurs and my inner permission is given. But does *no one else* have such experiences?

Today I watched some of my moves in the mirror. I saw an aura along the arms and shoulders. It was midway between red and purple—a new shade—not the intense red of so many years ago, or the deep magenta of more recent times. I realized I would *never* be able to perform these body *mudras* before others. My body has grown too slack and flabby with age, yet as Carol once said of sex, this is not a *visual* experience, anyway. Yet it is hard to believe that the *sound alone* begets these sensations. I think it is more. I think it is magic. I think I (or the intelligence within) knows it well.

I wonder if men in general are wary of this rapturous reaction because, for them, feeling itself tends to be suspect, and bodily pleasure centered in the genitalia. For women, physical delight is more diffuse, flowing throughout the system. They have less fear of feelings, of being overmastered or swept away, and can tolerate or welcome pleasant sensation anywhere, without guilt or fear of losing control. In general, women have accepted or approved of my response, and men have not.

Music and chanting continued to play a major role in my experience. For long periods, my morning practice focused on listening and moving to the chanting on Ram Dass' Chord of Love. *Later, I turned to Brahms'* German Requiem *and Bach's* Passion of St. Matthew. *Sacred music of whatever tradition affects me deeply. Sometimes I stood as quiet witness to the energies flowing within. Each experience was like an encounter with Divine Love.*

Here are some exercises I devised for myself several years ago near the beginning of my experience. They are simple, but as valid today as then:

For one day, respond to everyone you meet as if they were another version of yourself. When you look at their face, think of it as your face. Do not judge them. Do not think, "He is a bore," or "She is entertaining." Think only, "Here am I."

Breathing: Pay attention to your breath for one day. Breathe slowly in the morning. Breathe deeply all day. Do another deep breathing exercise at night.

Go into nature. Find a place to be still—see if you can "feel one" with the setting.

Try massage with a partner.

Meditate—with the idea of getting out of the way and feeling good.

Perform a self-massage on your face, head, feet, and hands.

Construct a personal myth of why you are here; for example, to help with the culture's "transitional period" as a volunteer.

Give time to self-analysis. What is your basic pattern? What lesson keeps coming up for you over and over?

Think about your progress in the process of individuation. How far have you come? Can you go too far, and end up reinforcing ego? What is false individuation?

Om: say this sacred syllable alone or with others.

Take every opportunity to participate in chanting. This is a very important practice.

A Dream of Mantras

Recently, I had a brief dream, in which two beings, one taller (older?) than the other (indeed, they were a somewhat mismatched pair) held their hands on my head and repeated mantras (or possibly only one mantra), whereupon I became aware of intricate, fantastic, geometrical designs or patterns. These were two-dimensional, but as if inscribed on a cloth or screen, and I realized that, given the right circumstances, I, too, have a visual imagination.

The Mystic Submission

Rapture, without defining doctrine, permits a unique purity of experience. One is not hampered by concerns of orthodoxy or ideological interpretation. Rather, one is, as one submits to the occasion; one is entered, infused, enraptured by a presence that one welcomes but does not seek to describe. Instead, one humbly acknowledges the arrival of the One.

Later, restored to a more familiar state, one ponders and questions. One reads "authorities," scans historical accounts, considers contemporary opinion, and from these derives a glimmer here, a suggestion there. But what, in fact, the experience ultimately is in its irreducible radiant core one never fully grasps, remaining poised forever at the edge of Mystery.

The Guises of Spirit

For purposes of transmission, not only the spirit, but the self, can assume any one of innumerable guises (guru and *chela*, spirit teacher and initiate, lover and beloved), choosing that which is most comfortable for the shared project. Thereafter, the two work in tandem under the selected identities, though other partnerships with different expressions may also serve.

Andrew Harvey Returns

Andrew Harvey has been back in San Francisco now for over two months. (He teaches here only intermittently.) I am auditing his class called "The Divine Mother in World Traditions." The first time I saw him after his return, he was on stage with others for a musical-dance-reading tribute to Rumi. I knew at once that something serious had happened. Has he been ill? I wondered. Has he had an accident?

I soon found out what was going on. The woman he had accepted as an avatar had rejected him, and he was no longer her disciple. At Christmas, he had taken Eryk, his beloved male partner, to her ashram, where he asked for her blessing on their union. She had refused to give it to him, and told him she did not approve of his lifestyle, given that he was her chief disciple and public spokesperson. She indicated that she wanted him to marry, and have children, so that the "transmission" could go forward.

Andrew was devastated. At a weekend workship in Santa Rosa, he poured out his feelings, his heartbreak, his sense of betrayal, his agony of spirit. He was extremely emotional in his revelation.

Many attending the workshop were bewildered and disturbed by his confession. Some had committed to this woman as a guru, and were confused and dismayed by the thought that she might not be worthy of their devotion. Some blamed Andrew for not being willing to give up his lifestyle. Some were angry that Andrew focused so intently on his personal situation at this workshop.

I was angry at her rejection of Andrew in his status as a gay man. It brought up all my feelings of betrayal and frustration from a lifetime of being made invisible in order not to offend others' sense of propriety.

His lectures in the class were, once again, brilliant, moving reflections of heart/mind wisdom. His aura has changed. I do not see the pale rainbow of colors of last year. Now I see deep, rich purple when he speaks.

My friendship with Andrew deepened through the years. I became increasingly impressed with this man, not only for his intellectual brilliance and charismatic charm, but for the depth and generosity of his spirit. I felt that meeting him had been indeed a gift of grace, for he was truly a "mirror of light."

Finding Others on the Path

In addition to Andrew and the other luminaries who had so impressed me, I also found many friends, who played significant roles in my life. One such was Helen, a fellow student I encountered in one of my classes. She was some twenty years younger than I—a yoga teacher and faithful adherent to dietary and other standards. Three of us from the class began to meet occasionally to discuss ideas and to give each other support in our respective life journeys. From the first, I had sensed Helen's electric energies, as if her spiritual pursuits had endowed her with a special vibration.

Then, one night, as she was speaking in our little group, I realized that her face was changing—she became someone else, a woman of a somewhat earlier time, with darker skin and hair, possibly Italian. Then as I continued to observe her, I saw her face go forward in time, as if years were slowly passing. Her features became full, her shoulders filled out, her hairstyle changed. Then, at the last, her face melted into old age, as the muscles sagged and shadows outlined her dimming countenance. In no way did I consciously recognize this person before me—yet I sensed on another level that she had once been a familiar companion, someone I had known and loved intimately at some other place and time.

Other unexpected events occurred in Helen's presence. She and I had walked out on the long pier near her house to observe the waves crashing ashore, roiled to a fury by the recent storm. As we watched, rainbows of color swept across the tops of the incoming waves at right angles to our vision. Each shot across some fifty to sixty feet or skipped from one incoming wave to the next. The Sun was just right that afternoon to catch this display in its full brilliance. It was the kind of moment that occurs only once. I wrote this poem about the experience:

Rainbows

As if the storm were not enough,
then there were rainbows.
Rainbows, not made of sky,
but fashioned from the waves' own sheen,
hued ribbons unfurling,
lilac, amber, blue,
flinging themselves across the line of spray
in arcs that streamed along the spume
like world horizons blown to color,
like energies of water sprites
released in shooting circling bands,
in some celebration we witnessed silently
not knowing then
what it was we were looking on,
or if we were meant to see.

My Chest Torn Open

It was Helen who had accompanied me on my venture into the "rapture of raptures," when I experienced such intense ecstasy before Baba Hari Dass, and it was she with whom I shared another of the most remarkable of my mystic adventures.

We had traveled with a small group to Mount Madonna for a weekend class in movement and the chakras. As one of the exercises, we were instructed to work in pairs. Helen and I were partners. Our instruction was to ask the partner a question, which she was to answer as if she were the deity Herself. Helen asked me her question, and I answered in some rather mundane fashion. Then it was my turn. I asked her, "What course should I pursue to enhance my spiritual growth?"

First, there was a long silence. I wondered why the answer did not come. Then I heard it—a sound that seemed to come from no one place in particular, not from Helen, but rather to emanate from the space around her. It was a single note, like the primordial Om which began the universe. My chest seemed to be torn open, with a rapture unequaled by any I had known previously. I could only silently bow my head in my concentrated effort to hold the moment. What was this power, and who was this mysterious being from whence it came?

Other Helpers

There were others who played a major role for me: Kit, herself a blossoming poet, with whom I shared my early efforts, and who became a treasured friend; Jan, who was keenly aware of world happenings, and yet amazingly tolerant of my own otherworldly inclinations. After listening to me describe kundalini happenings for years, she herself began to sense a radiant energy flow in her body during her free-form painting classes. Jouida, my astrologer friend, who constantly reminded us of the importance of the metaphysical realms. And Patricia, who decorated her walker in rainbow colors and named it the "wind-chime walker" after the small wind chimes she had hung on it. An artist and singer, she seemed to shower blessings wherever she went.

And of course Jeannine, artist, poet, kundalini compatriot, whom I met only once, at a kundalini conference (again, at the Mount Madonna Center), but who spoke to me often by phone of her ongoing unfoldment. ("Yesterday I saw the webs of light between my fingers, and last night when I woke up, I saw my husband's body ringed in light.") And Karen, to whom I could confess over the phone my many bizarre encounters, and who likewise could describe to me her own unique experiences.

All were part of a rich weave, a texture of friendship that sustained and inspired as we traveled together on our various related paths. San Francisco is indeed a magnet that draws those engaged in peripheral experience—all the ones who didn't fit in (and didn't want to) back home. This is the place where you can discover others of your kind, whatever your stripe or nature, even if you walk the sacred, invisible realms.

Walking in the Two Worlds

Perhaps my ecstasy is merely the right brain making love to the left.

It (the right brain) does not tell us things. It does not solve problems, add, subtract, analyze or sum up. It simply is as its own intense, simple, joyous self—a celebration of life that goes beyond the particular existence, that says, "Come join in the cosmic dance; it is not yours or mine or anyone's, but the blended performance of all that is from lowest to highest, from atom to God."

Ultimately, one must discover a way not to be overwhelmed by the experience, but rather to yield to it and acknowledge it as a sublime feature of one's own psyche. It is a continuing contest, thrust and parry, ebb and flow, the sudden flash flood of vision and the effort to integrate and comprehend. Constantly, we must turn up our limited receivers to admit higher and higher frequencies, to allow entry to ever more intense vibration streams from the infinite source.

The many universes exist simultaneously and are layered, one within the other, in the same space. Thus matter, light, and vibration yield worlds of physical, or electromagnetic, or spiritual reality all at the same time and place.

Everything is a dance of light and within that dance we find our world of appearances, our visual imagery, our sounds, our inner sensations. Underlying all is the source, which will speak to us and move us if we pause to attend.

Our small raptures are but minute tokens of the gods' ongoing cosmic bliss. Is God a state of perpetual cosmic rapture of which we are but brief microseconds of feeling? Is this our purpose, to contribute through our conscious presence to the deity's overwhelming cosmic spasms of delight? And does God also suffer pain commensurate with this bliss?

If we identify primarily with the aspect of transcendent suffering (as do many Christians), we welcome pain as purgation, and look as well for divine consolation and repair. If we identify with divine rapture, we crave always to be drowned in the holy flood. Can we accommodate both? Can we "dance in our own blood"? Can we know God both as healer and lover, as the source of the wound and also the ecstatic partner? Can we hold the polarities in our own body as God holds them in the world? Is the love-death the final end of all?

At this moment, more people are being plunged into suffering and more lifted into ecstasy than ever before. The boundaries are dissolving between state and state, level and level. The gates are opening. Can the dying know bliss in the midst of pain? Can the enraptured ones maintain their consciousness of universal agony? Can our familiar limits be extended as we pierce the boundaries of our experienced world? How much can the "merely human" sustain of greater concentration of both pleasure and pain until it lifts to become a new species, or collapses in chaos and decay?

On the one hand kundalini—rapture transcending the realm of the personal, with the latter's subjective entanglements and despair. On the other—traumas of terrorism, war, cancer, plague. Again, the personal is overridden, as forces of massive devastation rage across the planet. So, our world today is at once a theater of disaster and a stage for universal transfiguration. We are at once Christ hanging on the cross and the splendor of the reawakened self.

For some time, the now familiar process of pain alternating with acute bliss continued. Again and again, I thought I had achieved a point of balance, only to be brought down once more. But gradually the energies abated, becoming ever softer and more subtle, and the swings became less extreme. My many symptoms (stomach, eyes, etc.) began to diminish, with the help of body workers, supplements, herbs, and other remedies. I discovered others who had had comparable spiritual experiences, and personal accounts of kundalini were beginning to appear in print.

I realized, once again, that mine was not merely a private experience, but part of a larger universal process of planetary awakening, of bringing the body and spirit into an alignment with divine love unlike anything humanity had previously known. This, I sensed, was the moment in history we had awaited so long. I felt deeply privileged to be a participant in this difficult but immensely significant process of human transfiguration.

I had turned to spiritual poetry as a major writing outlet. It was Andrew Harvey (by now he and his husband Eryk were my treasured soul friends) who encouraged me, urging me to complete a volume of poems based on the voyage of discovery I had undertaken. Under Andrew's prodding and tutelage, I completed this book of sacred verse (titled Marrow of Flame: Poems of the Spiritual Journey)*, which was published in the spring of 2000 by Hohm Press.*

Surprisingly, this volume met with enthusiastic response from readers on many levels. In it many found mirror images of their own deepest experiences. Perhaps most important, through the book (and the tape of the poems, which Andrew recorded with me) I came in contact with others who were well into their own journeys of exploration and discovery. At last, I was no longer alone on my voyage. Together, all of us were moving into the new era of elevated consciousness and shifting planetary vibration. We needed no textual proofs, for we had confirmed in our own radical experience that massive changes were under way. We were the forerunners, the pioneers, the "planetary mystics"—together we were now "bringing the treasure home."

A Final Note

I am tired of qualms and questions—to publish or not to publish. The time for sharing is here; let this account find its own way in the world; let these words serve as their own justification.

Someone once advised me to wait to publish my story until the process was finished. But the journey is never completed. There is only constant death and renewal, repeated shattering of the self and reformation of the core, in the perpetual progression toward an unseen but deeply sensed destination.

I have done what I can, given what I have. I can only hope that as more and more share in this experience, these words will be of value to those who are experiencing, or witnessing, this key evolutionary event—the global awakening to kundalini and Divine Love.

Postscript

Recently, I participated with my women's circle (Sacred WomanSpace) in an impromptu healing ceremony. As we surrounded our sister in need of help and directed our love and affirmation toward her, I felt the sweet, intense energies of the group enter my chest and open my heart in a soft ecstasy, then flow out through my arms and hands toward our comrade. Oh, yes, I thought, this is what I have been needing, this is the way I have wanted it to be. Let this heavenly tenderness pour into us, then from all of us to one another, so that we may heal ourselves and each other, and ultimately the world in a vibrant outpouring of all encompassing love. How else can it happen?

Love Takes Us into its Holy Ground

Who was I, that such a thing
should happen.
An ordinary woman,
living an unremarkable life
until a presence appeared
a being from some other
place or planet not found on any map,
reality without an image or a name.

Then you entered me and stayed,
a constant element like blood throbbing
through a vein
or light flowing
through all the secret chambers
of the heart
each cell and particle awakened
by your relentless call.

Now I am a no thing
a naked enterprise of love,
a relic on a ravaged field
its essence swallowed by this clear light,
this transparent flaming joy.

Part 5

Afterword: Reflections on Kundalini, Enlightenment, and Other Matters

The Rishis

What they knew
was that life
is not a pure exposition
of darkness, or light,
but a compendium,
a constantly shifting
blend,
as if from a master of chiaroscuro
who wanted to try all
the possible combinations
and angles,
gradations and permutations
of depiction
before declaring balance,
and then not stasis,
but the delicate harmony
of chaos, where everything streams
each shifting molecule,
each flowing strand of transitoriness
straining toward fulfillment
not through gaudy symmetry
but from the hidden skein
of a tangled, crafty design.

What Is Kundalini?

Of all human phenomena, kundalini is one of the most mysterious and least understood. In ancient yogic texts, kundalini is imaged as a "serpent" resting at the base of the spine. When aroused, it ascends in spiral fashion through the various chakras ("wheels") of the body until it reaches the crown (the top of the head), where its energies unite with those of the immensity that sustains all. At that moment, the small self loses itself in forgetfulness, and regains its primal condition as part of the ever flowing consciousness that is the final reality. This—a state of unimaginable bliss—is known as enlightenment.

Kundalini means "coiled," for in the Hindu symbology the snake is coiled three and a half times in its resting place. According to traditional thought, each chakra is an energy center, a "wheel" that presumably begins to spin as the energy passes through it. On each side of the spinal column is a major channel for ascent, one known as *ida* and the other *pingala*. These form a helix around the central channel, the *sushumna*, a tiny thread rising from the base to the top of the spinal column.

Many devout students of yoga devote their lives to perfecting the technique of awakening and then lifting the kundalini energies. To this end, they adhere to a strict yogic discipline, including the practice of *asanas* (positions), a restricted diet, and performance of austere purification measures. Only the very pure in body and spirit are deemed fit to follow this path with impunity. Those less prepared expose themselves to dangers of every sort, from physical illness to emotional unbalance. Because of the difficulties inherent in the practice, the student is cautioned to proceed only under the guidance of an experienced teacher. Once the technique is mastered, the student is said to be gifted with many "supernatural" powers—such as the ability to see or hear at a distance, to travel out of body, and to charm without effort.

Kundalini has also played a prominent role in many other
cultures, where it has been a key element in spiritual practice.
Kundalini (under various names) has been identified as central
to such spiritual traditions as the esoteric practices of early Egypt,
Taoism in Asia, and shamanism throughout the world. Some feel
that even the ecstatic states reported in mystic Christianity
reflect the workings of kundalini. Kundalini, by whatever name,
is universally treasured as a sacred experience, and venerated as
a means of passage to other worldly realms.

In contemporary thought, kundalini is widely viewed as the
essential electromagnetic system that undergirds and sustains all
of the operations of the self, from physical to mental to emotional. This guiding force generally operates below the level of
consciousness, keeping the body in balance and performing in a
"normal" fashion. However, spontaneous kundalini experiences—even full awakening—can occur, and unexpected arousal
is being reported more and more frequently across the globe.
Oftentimes, the arousal occurs as a direct consequence of some
emotional or psychic shock to the system, as if a vacuum is created in the normal field of consciousness and kundalini rushes
forth to fill the gap. Other possible triggers are the experiences of
childbirth and death itself.

Further, the path of the arousal may vary from the traditional
descriptions. The energies may simply rush upward in a general
swift ascent, a possibility recognized even in certain ancient
accounts. As the process continues over time, the energies may
be felt as a diffuse bliss rather than as a progression through the
classic channels.

In the majority of cases, this "awakening" is imbued with a
deeply spiritual cast. It generally begets in the subject a response
of humility and awe. She is now able to experience states far transcending anything known before. It is as if she now thinks and
feels at the cellular level, with a capacity for knowing deeper and
swifter than any perception achieved through the familiar
rational mind. She may now be vulnerable to states of both
ecstasy and pain beyond any previously imagined. Some may

develop rare healing powers or acute mental abilities. In its perfect manifestation, kundalini purges the self of all its latent illness and psychological perturbation, leaving a being empowered to express her fullest potential.

Gopi Krishna maintained that kundalini would be the engine for the evolutionary transformation of humanity. Those who experience its high bliss and overwhelming sense of connectedness to divine purpose and direction can only concur. Whatever else it does, kundalini permanently changes the nervous system, making it capable of states of awareness well beyond the familiar spectrum. These changes lead to a shift not merely in *what* we see but *how* we see. The threshold is lowered for both pleasure and pain, the defenses are stripped away. One experiences the interconnectedness of all beings and levels in the most personal and intimate sense; one resonates at the deepest centers with this newfound knowledge.

Kundalini opens the system to infusions of the divine; one is held by unmitigated, unimaginable, pure love. And this love is the sustaining force of the cosmos itself.

This transition to a new state is not easy. Those refined energies appear to visit the forerunners, in effect, the "volunteers," those who have (it would seem) in some mysterious and undefined way agreed to undergo this process as part of the saving transformation of the race. Each one becomes a way station, a base of energetic force helping to sustain the ongoing process, which no one comprehends in its fullness but each feels honored to serve. Each participant gives in the manner best suited to personal talent or capacity. Perhaps the assignment is, as one friend put it, simply to "carry this vibration" until it can be established throughout the planet.

The path is without familiar precedent or guidance. Together, this collective (whose members are most often not known to one another) prepares a field of consciousness, which makes each subsequent transfiguration less difficult for those who follow. (Rupert Sheldrake uses the term "morphogenetic field" to describe such phenomena.) In the kundalini process the divine becomes dramatically aware of itself as being embodied in the human. Humanity is the device whereby the sacred reality establishes itself more firmly on Earth in fullest manifestation.

Kundalini as such is not a stranger to Earth. But our age is the first in which kundalini consciousness is coupled with the heightened self-awareness available to the contemporary mind. The intuitive and the rational (right-left brain functions) now may be paired in a new way. The body is known in a fresh perspective. The self becomes a ground for experiment; the mind experiences novelty and then reflects on its own internal operations.

The rapture awakened in many kundalini experiences is not to be confused with sexual arousal (though they are kin), nor are the reports of bliss to be dismissed as merely accounts of interesting internal somatic events. For the serious student, each such experience carries the sense of the infusion of the holy energies, a uniting with a force so beyond conceptualization that feeling itself is the only avenue of communication. Although we cannot know the divine reality in full, we can in part experience it in our bodies. Hence the paradox: we remain convinced of the reality of that which we can neither see nor hear, which lacks substance and material presence, but which nonetheless is our daily companion.

Because we in modern society typically do not experience kundalini under ideal conditions, we often must spend many years in the balancing process. Some become so sensitive that they may no longer be able to function in the familiar world, and must go into a period of retreat. Others may become highly creative and discover talents they did not know they possessed. Virtually all, however, agree that this is an experience to be prized above all others, for it endows the recipient with an irrefutable sense of deep connection to that which is most meaningful in human experience.

One feels that there is indeed a divine presence, and knows that one is in fact very much a part of that reality, however minute or humble one's role. This is unconditional love in its most compelling expression. It is the final proof, the assurance that goes beyond all doubts and questionings, the ultimate self-validating experience. It is the path to "planetary initiation," an entry into a new mode of being.

In Retrospect

I think it not possible to write of kundalini apart from the total life. It is the experience that is the distillation of all earlier experiences, the iridescent tincture that remains at the bottom of the dish when the dross has been burned away. It is the essence and the proof, marrow and primal substance. To try to speak of it isolated from the rest would be like pulling a brilliant thread from a tapestry, the better to understand its role in the total composition.

All of life is, I think, initiation, and initiation upon initiation. Constant death and returning, endless relinquishment and renewal. Kundalini is one such vivid cycle, but so was one's first day at school, at the time the single most challenging and significant event yet experienced. The final initiation, of course, is that which swings us out of life (on this plane) and into death. In the meantime, we progress, always striving to integrate the leaf that has newly unfolded, into the existing design.

The Moment That Changes Everything

Katherine Anne Porter, speaking of her near-death experience during the great influenza epidemic of World War I, said that this was an event that irretrievably changed her life. Before that, everything was a preparation, getting ready. Afterward, she was ready, prepared. But she was not the same as other people. She could no longer live as they did, making their decisions, living in ordinary, familiar ways.

Such is the nature of the overwhelming moment. It changes not only the future, but reshapes, restructures the very past. Everything which *was* is seen as mere preliminary, a cause serenely unfolding its climactic effect, contributory streams at last mingling with a roar into the major channel, which at once is ourselves and the medium that sweeps us forward.

The experience can come in many forms—mystical vision, physical ecstasy, the soul's dark night from abrupt or accumulated loss. Whatever its contours, it opens us to the new self, the being now refashioned as a revised instrument to receive life's charge. At its height, the moment tells us that we have transcended ordinary experience, have met and fused with deity, even. There is temporary comfort in that thought. Rapture itself is confirmation of an ultimate, benign source, to which one has only to conform to partake of its blissful essence. The experience serves as proof of its own reality. One knows in silence, requiring no commentary or validating argument.

Yet, always, at every moment except the peak, there is a question. How do we know that the entire phenomenon is not produced from some subjective stratagem, some trick of imagination or bodily chemistry deluding us by its unaccustomed effects? How can we recognize what stands outside all prior experience? Indeed, how can we be sure that the reputed paradise opening to receive us at death is not another dream, more compelling but composed of the same mind stuff as our ordinary night fictions? Are we truly "out-of-body" or do we but imagine the severance of psyche from source? Is risen kundalini proof of cosmic energy lifting us into divine union, or a trick of the nervous system, an esoteric aberration arising out of peculiar breathing and concentration?

The happening and its classic interpretation are not of necessity congruent. An ecstasy in the head is not ultimate proof of the presence of God. A sensation of petals opening does not itself confirm the attainment of the bodhisattva state. We move to a new level, but nothing reveals its ultimate nature, only that it is a departure from our past experience.

Yet—what saying or insight finally contradicts our experience? Though we cannot interpret it fully by mind, we know that we have been irrevocably transformed. Having seen, we cannot erase the lingering inner image. Having felt, we cannot deny the force which has swept through us, cleansing and renewing, confirming that we are more than we know, and that we know more than we can utter.

So we are left once more with the eternal paradox, that the experience which is least interpretable is most compelling, and that to reduce transcendence to "nothing but" explanations robs the event of its power, and denies the reality of that which we have confirmed in the fires of our own inner rituals.

Once, when I was a child of eleven or so, I was playing at twilight with other children in the backyards of the neighborhood. It was a game of running and hiding. I was flying across a dim lawn, in my child's wild delight of free movement, when, from somewhere in the gathering dark, a mesh wire fence caught me at the chest, stopping me in midstride. I felt betrayed, ambushed by hostile forces. I dropped out of the game, went indoors to nurse my bruises, most evident across my small breasts, which were just beginning to emerge.

How rapturous had been my flight. How abrupt and terrifying its termination, the more so because the fence had risen invisibly from a malevolent darkness to confound me. So it is, when we seek to penetrate the absolute by logic and reason, to gather speed until we shunt forward into the unknown. We run our poor bodies (or psyches) against an unseen barricade, a prohibiting lattice where we had supposed only space, which effectively blocks our flight and hurls us back into the bitter province of the mundane, our familiar reality.

The Most Secret Experience

Of all experiences of the inner self, kundalini is the most secret, the most protected. It is the most intimate, the most personal. One does not wish to speak of it because to do so is, as it were, to reveal sacred knowledge, to expose secrets divulged in private to the single listener. Kundalini brings us in direct confrontation with that which we are, our quintessential, fundamental self—that range of sensation and patterned feeling, the memory of which we long ago buried in the depths below consciousness, but which occasionally surfaced, briefly and in disguise, in moments of intense feeling.

But once reencountered, we know it immediately as our very selves, the stranger we have yearned to meet, the god we have sought to know. It confirms the familiar assertion, so often challenged or denied—we and the god are one.

To describe the sensation of kundalini is like delineating the course of sexual arousal. Can one adequately convey to another in words that which is experienced in the realm of pure sensation? I think not. It is personal, unique, part of the individual repertoire of response. By listening to *my* account of *my* experience, you may, possibly, relate it to something in your own sphere and judge it to be similar or not. But you can never know the true quality of my subjective response unless you *become* me or, like a spirit, enter my system in order to taste with my mouth, sense with my nerves.

But kundalini is far more than a sensation. It is at once an awakening, a recognition, and a call. The awakening is into awareness of that which before was merely reputed, but is now confirmed. The recognition is of an inner process and response at once new and familiar, whether from this life or another. The call is to deal with it, integrate it, and then carry its energy forward into a new enterprise. To ignore it is to turn one's back on God.

How meager is our vocabulary when we refer to pleasurable physical/mental experience. We can speak of what is joyous, blissful, rapturous, ecstatic, orgasmic, even. But after that, words fail. To know more, we must enter the realm of experience, for knowledge can come only from the event, not from its descriptors. The account of the experience is like a report relayed to the back lines from advance scouts up ahead. The description of the mountain is not the same as being one with the mountain. To know the mountain, one must go into its presence.

What Is Enlightenment?

Enlightenment occurs when we (the inner being) abdicate the awareness and concerns of the local self and merge completely with the larger universal consciousness. This union can be achieved only through the abandonment of ordinary thought processes, and entry into ecstatic awareness of being as such (bliss). This is accomplished through the release of the kundalini energies, which travel through the system, opening the body to its fullest receptivity, and culminating in the embrace of Shiva/Shakti at the crown. Then, and then only, one knows one's essence and source—divine, intoxicating, universal energy. At that moment, the rest is irrelevant.

For an instant, one transcends the polarities. Now comes a choice: to remain "forever" in blissful union—or to return to the world of the antimonies, with its conflicts and bitterness, its sufferings and confusions.

The latter is the only valid option in our time. One comes back to this world in order to do one's bit, to aid the project one feels is in progress, to participate in the global shift of consciousness so many describe. One thus hovers between the two worlds, in a difficult posture. One is now open to the cosmic forces—as energy, as delight, as ultimate being (for one returns many times to the original moment of awakening), but one also travels daily among the turbulence or apathy of the "unawakened" world.

There one is subject to constant buffeting and assault—and must struggle to maintain composure and equilibrium amid the strife. Sometimes one almost envies the unawakened—those whose nerves and intellect are bounded and secure by their state of unknowing. But in one's heart of hearts, one knows one has chosen the right course, has made the only possible choice.

Dealing with the Critic Within

Early practitioners, no doubt, lived their ecstasy free from the disturbing intrusions of the critical mind. There was no need to question the validity of their experience. Ecstasy was not suspect. They could easily fit personal experience into a cosmic scheme. The recluse, the hermit—these simply disengaged from the chaos of the societal arena. They had no need to interact with the world on its own terms, to explain, or to defend. They were free to pursue their inner bliss, without explanation or apology.

Ours is not so easy a task. We are (many of us) deeply steeped in the critical mode, ready to place even the most intimate or exalted moment of inner experience up for inspection. We wish to know not merely what has happened, but why. Often we become our own most severe critics. We challenge our most transcendental experiences, dismissing them as mere self-hypnosis or temporary delusion. We question our discoveries of sacred connection as mere longing for the lost bliss of the womb. We challenge and diminish, reduce and explain. We are so afraid of trickery that we ourselves become the most flagrant tricksters, employing every stratagem or approach that will offer explanation and relieve us of the burden of mystery.

In effect, we walk in two worlds. One is the realm of the ordinary, of consensus reality, where rules and explanations and agreed-upon codes prevail. The other is private to the point of being unique. It is neither shared nor open to external verification. It is the ultimate subjective, the personal realm that does not seek to impose its tenets on others (it has none) or to influence by conscious intent the life of society moving around it. Its precepts cannot be challenged, because they arise from experience, not assumptions. The conclusions of this subjective process cannot be invalidated because it has none to offer. It simply is: an untestable anomaly in the contemporary world, perhaps a flashback to a time when human consciousness was more susceptible to inner movement, less self-conscious in its explorations of the intimate, personal realms.

So we practice, bringing Shakti into ecstatic union with Shiva, feeling the vibrations of the mantra reverberate blissfully throughout our bodies, discovering in movement, in breath, these rapturous realms of the sacred. At these moments, we do not care what the inner skeptic says. We lay aside the reflective mind in order to enter the private realm where human and divine connect, where the sacred abides. Once more, we experience sanctity. Once again, we enter the precincts of the holy.

Thus we proceed, vacillating between two realms, one the world of common perception and the other that of transcendent vision. We seek to unify the disparates, left brain/right brain; rational, intuitive; mind/body. To commit fully to one or the other would be a relatively easy task. But we are the shock troops of evolution, ourselves the field on which the pageant is played, our own unified awareness the prize to be shared by the new species now coming into being.

On Kundalini and the Sacred

With the increase in reported kundalini phenomena, many investigations are attempting to reduce the experience to a "nothing but" event: to a measurable psycho-physiological play of the nervous system; to a series of symptoms ranging from the bizarre to the psychotic; to a singular component of a larger delusional syndrome.

Kundalini may include aspects of any or all of the above. It may bring with it curious readjustments of the psyche as well as the bionetwork; it may trigger a passing symptomatology both unfamiliar and disturbing; it may awaken deep memory, buried racial and archetypal themes. But kundalini is far more than an electromagnetic impulse; it is not merely another pathology of mind or body; it is based on something far more profound than delusion.

Kundalini is well documented as part of the practice of seekers in ancient times, and today, kundalini is one of the last remaining instruments we possess for entry into the world of the sacred. It is the unimaginably powerful agent for putting us—we, the intellectually sophisticated ones of the contemporary world—in touch with those lost realms in which our ancestors dwelt in intimate relation with an unseen but powerful reality.

Kundalini is aptly compared to a snake that bites as it rises. It conveys us quickly into the heart of the self-validating experience. It is a feeling, not an assertion, and thus because it is experienced with such fullness and finality at the core of being, we acknowledge that it needs no confirmation through ordinary rational procedures. This is not to say that we do not ask, "What is this mysterious power?" or seek to discover the secrets of its origin and its mode of operation. But beyond these discernible physio-logical facts, or the electromagnetic observations, emerges a body of evidence, nonmeasurable, unweighed, yet of infinite intensity and conviction. Like the aesthetic response, it carries a convincingness beyond the explainable. Like the mystic moment, it rests within the assurance of its own ineffable reality.

What, then, is kundalini? Most immediately, it is an experience of the body/spirit that yields bliss not accessible to the ordinary senses. This moment of transcendent rapture carries with it con-viction of union with that which exists beyond the self. It confirms, however transitorily, that we, as conscious beings, are part and par-cel of a larger reality whose outlines and composition we can but barely guess. For that time, words, pronouncements, the idle chat-ter within, are suspended. We are, as the cliché has it, "at one with the infinite." We have heard these words too many times to accept them without challenge. Yet, simple and shopworn as they are, they tell us of our perennial yearning to connect—to *join*—to locate and consciously merge with our original source, which we may not accurately name but whose presence stirs in us perpetually.

Kundalini opens the gates to that sacred space. One who seeks access to these precincts merely to probe or gauge or meas-ure will miss its identifying features entirely. He might as well cut open the heart to locate the seat of the soul, or explore the essence of matter merely by reducing a substance into finer and finer particles. This one will discover no spirit guide, no sacred groves. Like the investigator who seeks to explore with a lantern the nature of darkness, he will drive before him the evidence he seeks. For him the charms will fail, the alchemy falter. He lacks the language of this foreign territory, and hence will never unlock its meaning or capture its truth.

Reminders of the Shadow

To complete initiation, we must discover a way—or become possessed by a way—to reconcile the opposites. Yet, all around us, on personal and transpersonal levels, in private and cosmic realms, the evidence piles up that the split widens, moving toward a seemingly irreconcilable rift.

Consider bliss and the shadow. I have known a good deal of bliss in my life. In meditation, movement, group energy experiences, yoga, breathing, holding still, a rapture flows. I am "ravished by the god," I enter a realm of such deep sensuous delight, I forget that I am a mortal, subject to the contingencies of the everyday. I become *nothing but bliss awareness*. I am bliss; bliss is my self and substance.

But then I awaken. I come back to "reality" and find myself, once again, in California, at the center of ever recurring catastrophe. Here the ground roars and opens beneath your very feet; giant sheets of fire incinerate not just houses but people, neighborhoods, entire communities, cars pile up in massive collisions on fog-darkened freeways.

And all around us is evidence of such individual suffering as we had not dreamt of. Mothers with children in arms beg in the street, human wrecks huddle on sidewalks, old women wrap themselves in blankets against the cold as they curl up in doorways.

The indecencies of government and various national and international institutions are too familiar to catalog. Foreign powers attack us with terrifying weapons of destruction. Powerful commercial interests poison air, water, or soil, as common citizens wonder what to do; these same interests loot the national treasury through various schemes. We feel threatened on all sides.

So it goes. Evidence of the Shadow, of universal disintegration of values and behavior, of recurrent disaster, is massive on all levels, personal, public, and cosmic. Each day reveals its new scenario of grief, of suffering, of massive corruption and decay. Yet each time we return to that deep center, each instant we make contact with that something which convinces us that we have not yet discovered who we truly are, we are filled again with a bliss which whispers of that which exists beyond suffering. We know we are linked to an inscrutable power that pervades our consciousness and carries our body to near insupportable levels of rapture. We feel that here, in this way, abiding in this reality, once again we verify the ever present bond between human and divine, world and source.

A New Mode of Being

According to Ilya Prigogine, systems brought to a higher and higher level of stress will ultimately spring to a new, more complex, level of organization, or else disintegrate entirely. Many signs indicate we are approaching such a moment.

What then are our chances for such a leap—a propulsion into a new consciousness, given the current strains within the common psyche? What form might such a dramatic transformation take? What new creatures will emerge as "us"?

We could, theoretically, abdicate the realm of the material entirely, becoming creations composed of and dwelling solely in the realm of the energies. Considerable evidence exists for the existence of nonlocal consciousness, such as out-of-body experience, ESP, clairvoyance, the shared intuitive and psychic experiences of twins. This shucking of the mortal casement would presumably relieve us (the community) of many of our current social problems, such as universal suffering, violence, hunger, greed, and others. Where there is nothing to covet, there is nothing to seize. Tyranny is impractical in a realm where possessions do not exist and domination is not possible. We would, presumably, float about in radiant circles of light, free of threat or dangers. But how would our lives find focus? Toward what state or achievement would we strive? Is unbroken harmony the condition we desire?

Or we might retain the familiar material veil, but with some sort of massive infusion of a new, transcendent principle or perspective into the society at large. This would be a grandiose and comprehensive conversion of our very way of perceiving (sensing, knowing, reacting to) the world around us. Perhaps it would be produced by a dramatic overhaul of the nervous system, possibly through widespread awakening of kundalini power, all conceivably triggered by astrological alignments sending new frequencies into the Earth's atmosphere. Or perhaps such "seed beings," selves already experiencing and issuing the new frequencies, are already among us, awakening by their very presence others who will in turn resonate to the new frequencies.

Evolution occurs not in a state of tranquility but in times of acute stress and crisis. Our crisis is upon us. The outcome remains to be seen.

Transformation All Around

I am a listener. I listen to people's stories of those things that have changed their lives. Most specifically, I am interested in how consciousness itself shifts with new experience, opening awareness to dimensions unknown and unguessed.

What I have found (and statistics confirm this conclusion) is that an astonishing number of people—educated, rational, balanced—are having experiences of the "incredible." These breaks in the norm are occurring not just in the enclaves of the initiates (Findhorn, Crestone) but seemingly everywhere—in the Midwest as well as the avant-garde West Coast, among the nonbelievers as well as the converted.

An avowed skeptic undergoes acupuncture for pain alleviation, and in the first session experiences a mystical revelation; she sees the shimmering net of energy that comprises and binds together all reality. A graduate student becomes chronically ill, and finds that her body is now so charged that she affects the energy fields (stops clocks, cuts electrical power) wherever she goes. A professor decides to enter another's body (psychically) to grasp more fully the experience of one denied full membership in the larger society. The next day, he finds that the "other" (who knew nothing of the experiment) carries seeming burn marks on his arms, and reports that something happened to him that was "very purifying." Someone is lost in a strange city in Asia, and has neither map nor language skills to find her destination. She "projects" herself mentally over the route to the desired goal, then follows it to make a timely (physical) arrival. These are not accounts contained in someone's study or book. They are all experiences that have been related to me quite recently.

Yes, something is happening, and not everyone needs a "mind-blowing" rave experience or a drug trip or even a guru to reach the next level. This is the actual quantum leap, the sudden transit from one orbit to the next without crossing the intervening space.

Despite the noise that surrounds this emerging phenomenon—certain glamorous channels with their stables of high-priced thoroughbreds, certain gurus with their Cadillacs and their scandals, the false prophets eager to bestow a speedy enlightenment for ready cash—something *real* is taking place and we should acknowledge it and welcome it as it leads us toward who we truly are.

The next stage in human evolution is to open up more fully to what we already possess, to contact more deeply what we already know. If we can, sitting in our living rooms in Kansas, suddenly feel our heads open in delight as exquisite energy flows in from an undetectable cosmic source, then what is not possible? My friend Carol had commented that this event (mine), given the location and improbable circumstances under which it occurred, must have been a "cosmic joke." Well, the cosmic joker is out and about, and the play is constantly in motion to bring us at last to ourselves so that we can know, if not the end, at least the right direction and next stage of our journey.

Glossary

Ashram: a spiritual community or institution where students study yogic wisdom and practices under the guidance of a *guru* (teacher).

Bhajan: a devotional song or chant.

Bhakta: one who seeks the Divine through love and devotional practice.

Bhakti yoga: that path which emphasizes devotion as a primary route to God.

Chakra (literally "wheel" or "circle"): an energy center in the subtle body through which the power of Consciousness manifests reality; center of consciousness. The major *chakras* along the spine correspond to the primary nerve plexuses (networks) in the physical body. In ancient lore, these "wheels" were thought to turn as the energy passed through. The number of major *chakras* is most often given as seven, though the number may vary. There are also minor *chakras* located in various other parts of the subtle body such as the hands or feet.

Crown chakra: the *chakra* located at the top of the head. When the *kundalini* enters the *sahasrara,* the spiritual center of the crown of the head, the individual self merges with the universal Self and attains the state of Self-realization.

Darshan: seeing a saint, holy being, or an image of the Divine.

Guru: spiritual teacher.

Ida: the *nadi* that rises on the left side of the body. It starts on the left and ends on the left, but crosses back and forth with the *pingala nadi* as they intersect at the major *chakras.* The intertwined dual snakes on the caduceus is a symbol of the *ida* and *pingala nadis* crossing back and forth over the *sushumna,* the straight central *nadi.*

Kirtan: devotional singing or chanting, often in *Sanskrit.*

Kundalini (literally "snake," "coiled"): the cosmic energy or evo-lutionary force that rests at the base of the spine of each being. It is metaphorically imaged as a snake that rises when awakened, and hence is referred to as the "serpent power." A fully ascended kundalini will produce a state of ecstatic iden-tification with the Self.

Krishna: an incarnation of God who is the most celebrated deity of the Hindu pantheon.

Mantra: a word or phrase imbued with sacred power. Often the name of a deity.

Maya: the veiling of reality by the limitation and differentiation of the phenomenal world.

Nadis: the channels of the subtle body through which the *prana* moves.

Nirvana: the transcendence of thought and language, of feeling and imagination, and of the ego-personality as a whole. Enlightenment.

Pingala: The *nadi* that rises on the right side of the body.

Prana (literally "breath"): cosmic energy that moves through the subtle body, governed in part by the breath process.

Puja: a devotional ritual.

Root chakra: the *chakra* at the very base of the spine, where one aspect of kundalini sleeps until it is awakened and brings the individual to the awareness of their unity with the Divine; the other aspect of kundalini is always functioning to create and support our embodied existence.

Samadhi: a meditative, superconscious state in which the fluc-tuation of the mind ceases. Last stage of yoga in which the final identification is reached.

Samsara: the deceptive world of changing appearance.

Shakti: the primal energy, personified as the goddess Shakti, who is the consort of Shiva. Out of love Shakti gives countless forms to her transcendent formless partner, which we experience as the universe.

Shiva: the third god of the major Hindu trinity. The symbol of higher consciousness. The transcendent divine principle.

Sushumna: the central channel *(nadi)* of the subtle body, which extends from the root *chakra* to the crown *chakra*. In the classic model, the kundalini travels through this *nadi* to the *sahasrar,* the crown *chakra* near the top of the head.

Subtle body: the superphysical body, including the mental self, the emotional self, and the channels *(nadis)* that carry the *pranic* energy.

Tantra: an esoteric system for awakening the subtle energies of the body as a means of achieving divine union. The feminine principle (Goddess) is central to this practice. May or may not occur in a specifically sexual context. The *tantric* tradition is based on the fact that all love, all bliss, all consciousness arise solely from Universal Consciousness, from the Self. *Tantra* is focused on experiencing the Divine in every moment, in every aspect of life.

Yantra: a sacred design for meditation, contemplation, and devotion.

Suggested Readings and Additional Resources

Books

Adler, Janet. 1995. *Arching Backward: A Mystical Initiation of a Contemporary Woman.* Rochester, Vermont: Inner Traditions. The author's lengthy process of spiritual awakening, including many archetypal inner visions.

Avalon, Arthur (Sir John Woodroffe). 1974. *The Serpent Power: The Secrets of Tantric and Shaktic Yoga.* New York: Dover Publications. Originally published in 1919, this work presents translations and discussion of two esoteric Sanskrit texts from several centuries previous. A work of profound scholarship, it is difficult, yet can be extremely rewarding to the serious student.

Bentov, Itzhak. 1977. *Stalking the Wild Pendulum.* Rochester, Vermont: Destiny Books. Offers an intriguing theory as to the possible physiological basis of kundalini experiences.

Degler, Teri. 1996. *The Fiery Muse: Creativity and the Spiritual Quest.* Toronto: Random House of Canada. Reveals the links between creativity, spiritual unfoldment, and the evolution of consciousness.

Edwards, Lawrence. 2000. *The Soul's Journey: Guidance from the Divine Within.* iUniverse.com, Inc., or from Internet and standard booksellers. This Jungian/transpersonal therapist and yogic authority offers a moving account of his personal awakening, along with extremely valuable information on the kundalini process. His website, www.thesoulsjourney.com, also contains essential information.

Greenwell, Bonnie. 1990. *Energies of Transformation: A Guide to the Kundalini Process*. Cupertino, California: Shakti River Press. Particularly helpful as a reference guide. Includes detailed descriptions of kundalini symptoms, case histories, and cross-cultural information.

Kason, Yvonne, M.D., and Teri Degler. 1994. *A Farther Shore*. Toronto: HarperCollins. Inspiring discussion of the spiritual journey, including kundalini awakening.

Krishna, Gopi. 1971. *Kundalini: The Evolutionary Energy in Man*. Boulder, Colorado: Shambhala. This classic account describes the most famous kundalini experience in modern history.

Mookerjee, Ajit. 1982. *Kundalini: The Arousal of the Inner Energy*. New York: Destiny Books. Offers a traditional yogic perspective on the chakras and kundalini. Includes fine illustrations.

Sannella, Lee, M.D. 1987. *The Kundalini Experience*. Lower Lake, California: Integral Publishing. One of the first to recognize and research the many indications of kundalini arousal.

St. Romain, Philip. 1991. *Kundalini Energy and Christian Spirituality: A Pathway to Growth and Healing*. New York: Crossroad Publishing. Offers a readable and useful account of personal awakening from a Roman Catholic perspective.

Underhill, Evelyn. 1955. *Mysticism*. New York: The Noonday Press. This classic, detailed account of the stages of the mystical journey can be an extremely useful guide for the modern seeker, including those undergoing kundalini transformation.

Walters, Dorothy. 2000. *Marrow of Flame: Poems of the Spiritual Journey*. Prescott, Arizona: Hohm Press. This book was inspired by and reflects the stages of the kundalini experience as part of the soul's quest for its true identity.

Websites

Many websites and discussion groups are listed under:
Kundalini Websites and Discussion Groups
http://groups.yahoo.com/search?query=Kundalini
Some of the most helpful are the following:

Shared Transformation http://members.aol.com/ckress/st.html
This invaluable resource, formerly a newsletter, has aided countless spiritual explorers to find their way. Site includes valuable articles and discussion, as well as an extensive bibliography of books relating to kundalini. Sun Chariot Press, P.O. Box 5562, Oakland, CA 94605; e-mail: Ckress@aol.com.

Kundalinigateway http://www.list-server.net/kundalini
An extremely useful resource, which offers an extensive list of available websites dedicated to kundalini, as well as links listed by specific topic, such as general descriptions, the awakening process, personal accounts, and more.

Spiritweb http://www.spiritweb.org
A comprehensive source for spiritual information, including many entries devoted to kundalini.

SacredKundalini
http://groups.yahoo.com/group/sacredKundalini/join
An extremely helpful discussion site, for members to describe personal experiences, exchange suggestions, and generally communicate with others on the path.

Kundalini Mailing List
http://www.list-server.net/kundalini/index.html
A comprehensive site for dialogue and exchange. Includes essays, poetry, and bibliography, as well as a subscriber discussion group.

Kundalini Research Network http://www.kundalininet.org
This key organization, dedicated to the furtherance of research on the kundalini experience, also publishes a

newsletter and sponsors meetings at which members can share information and experiences with one another. (914-241-8510) c/o Lawrence Edwards, Ph.D., 66 Main St., Bedford Hills, NY 10507; e-mail: kundaliniresearc@netscape.net.

Kundalini Resource Center http://hmt.com/kundalini
Contains interesting and valuable information on various aspects of kundalini.

Kundalini Survival and Support http://kundalini-support.com
This site offers a wealth of invaluable information.

Spiritual Emergence Network http://www.senatciis.org/
Long a major referral and support center for persons under-going spiritual transformation, now based at the California Institute for Integral Studies in San Francisco. (415) 648-2610; or sen@ciis.edu.

About the Author

Dorothy Walters lives and writes in San Francisco. She recently published her first volume of poetry entitled "Marrow of Flame: Poems of the Spiritual Journey" (Hohm Press). Her primary interest is helping others undergoing spiritual transformation. She is available for poetry readings and talks and welcomes questions pertaining to kundalini awakening. Her e-mail address is dwalters2@worldnet.att.net.